M000307168

OTHER WORKS BY JEAN KLEIN

Be Who You Are
Who Am I?
Beyond Knowledge
Living Truth
Open to the Unknown
Transmission of the Flame
The Ease Of Being

Translations also available in French, Spanish, Italian, German and Chinese

I
AM

Jean Klein

compiled and edited by Emma Edwards

NON-DUALITY PRESS

Jean Klein Foundation
PO Box 22045
Santa Barbara, CA 93120
United States

jkftmp@aol.com
http://www.jean klein.org

First published 1989 by Third Millennium Publications
This edition copyright © Non-Duality Press
August 2006 & 2007
Copyright © Emma Edwards

All rights reserved. No part of this book may be reproduced, stored
in a retrieval system, or transmitted by any means, electronic,
mechanical, photocopying, recording, or otherwise, without
express written permission from the publisher.

ISBN 978-0-9551762-7-2

Non-Duality Press
Salisbury SP2 8JP
United Kingdom
www.non-dualitybooks.com

PREFACE

Some of you who read this book may have a kind of dèjâ-vu in places. This is because an earlier work *Neither This Nor That I Am* (Watkins 1981) has been completely revised and woven into these pages. I felt the earlier work needed re-writing; this book *I Am* is a clearer pointer to truth.

J.K

FOR THE READER

I am a mother. I am a son. I am a doctor. I am a lawyer. I'm musical. I'm tall. I'm short. I'm American. I am French. I am Jewish. I am Christian. I am black. I'm gay. I am celibate. I'm depressed. I'm happy. I'm married. I am this. I am that.

We know ourselves only in relation to something. We only know a qualified "I." When we say "I am" the mind demands "What am I? I am what?" This book is about the "I am" prior to all qualification, what we are before the intrusion of the mind.

How can we know what cannot be qualified? It calls for a new kind of knowing, not a knowledge which comes from the accumulation of facts and experience. We may have absorbed every book published and experienced every adventure and it would not bring us one breath nearer to knowing "I am." So this new knowing begins by giving up looking for it in experiences and secondhand information. Giving up does not mean we become passive; on the contrary, in letting go of our mechanical learned responses we are open to our full potential, our creativity, a dynamic new realm. The natural state of the relaxed brain is multidimensional attention. It does not need viewpoints, data, opinions, memory to be alert. When all these directions cease, an organic, non-directed wakefulness remains. This is the threshold of "I am."

This book is therefore about that which cannot be represented, objectified. It is about our real nature, truth, a truth that has nothing to do with the accumulation of facts. It is causeless, autonomous and only in this sense real. It needs no agent to be known and is its own proof. It is not having knowledge but immediate knowledge, knowing as being, and as such is not objectifiable. It is closer to us than all thought or feeling. It is our fundamental ground.

Since the "I am" is not an abstract, a concept or idea, the teaching of this truth is not a transmission of conceptual knowledge. The understanding of these dialogues does not occur in the mind. Of course the words, acting on the verbal level, bring the mind to greater clarity so that it has a clear geometrical representation of what is beyond it and also realizes the boundaries of its comprehension. But the fullness and real significance of these words lies in the fact that they do not arise from thinking but from the silence behind thought, the "I am." The answers appear in this silence, the openness that is present in the absence of a personal entity, and they are permeated with "the perfume" of their source. In this lies their transformative power: they arise out of and point to our real nature, our autonomy, at every moment. They are thus a constant challenge, a challenge to belief, education and common sense. They free us from the reflex to take ourselves for a somebody, a thinker, a seeker, a doer, a sufferer.

If these sayings are not meant to be comprehended in the usual sense of the word, by the mind; if we are not to bring our past knowledge and experience to bear on the interpretation, how should we read this book?

As we read poetry. When reading poetry we don't look for agreement or disagreement, the critical mind is suspended in order to let the impact of the poem make itself felt. When we read poetry, we are poets. We remain passively alert, letting the words be active, listening to how they echo on every level, how they sound, how they move in us, how we are moved by them. We wait attentively, without conclusion, for the poem to find us. This alert openness to all the resonances of the psychosomatic structure is vital to the truth-seeker. Like the poet, the truth-seeker lets go of his personality so that he is open to thoughts, feelings and reactions. Like the poet, the truth-seeker welcomes these as gifts, as pointers in the exploration.

Only in this openness can the silence in the words come home to us, for openness is the "I am," our real nature. The words are merely a catalyst to the real formulation which takes place in the reader.

E.E.

$\mathcal{W}$e must investigate, get to know ourselves, what we generally understand to be our body and psyche. Most of the time we live in reaction and double reaction, for example, when we react in anger we may also try to remain calm and collected. We try many different escape routes. By such means we constantly limit our possibilities and turn in a vicious circle.

The only way out is to simply observe. This allows us to take note of our physical reactions, our mental attitudes and patterns and our motivations at the exact moment they appear. It involves no evaluation, no analysis which is based on memory. At first the observer might find it difficult to be impersonal, to free himself from evaluating. He tends to emphasize the object and thus become its accomplice. Later, however, observing itself is emphasized and becomes more natural, more frequent. There comes a time when a neutrality installs itself between the observer and what he observes, and both poles lose their driving force. There is silence, we no longer nourish the conditioned object.

What is the primary motivation for our actions?

At certain moments, when alone, we feel a great lack deep within ourselves. This lack is the central one giving rise to all the others. The need to fill this lack, quench this thirst, urges us to think and act. Without even questioning it, we run away from this insufficiency. We try to fill it first with one object then with another, then, disappointed, we go from one compensation to another, from failure to failure, from one source of suffering to another, from one war to another. This is the destiny to which a large part of humanity devotes itself. Some resign themselves to this state of being which they judge to be inevitable. Others at first deluded by the satisfaction brought about by these objects come to realize that they give rise to a surfeit and even to indifference. Some are brought to take a closer look. The object fully satisfies us for a short time during which we are back in our intrinsic nature, fulfillment. At the moment of fullness there is no awareness of an object. Thus the object cannot be the cause of our experience. It is essential to come to know these moments of joy without object.

We habitually attribute a cause to joy, we turn joy into an object because memory links the two together, but in reality they are of two entirely different natures. Thus we realize that the object is consumed in the joy of our being.

Is it true that when we look at our surroundings from silent awareness they find their natural state of harmony?

It is only through silent awareness that our physical and mental nature can change. This change is completely spontaneous. If we make an effort to change we do no more than shift our attention from one level, from one thing, to another. We remain in a vicious circle. This only transfers energy from one point to another. It still leaves us oscillating between suffering and pleasure, each leading inevitably back to the other. Only living stillness, stillness without someone trying to be still, is capable of undoing the conditioning our biological, emotional and psychological nature has undergone. There is no controller, no selector, no personality making choices. In choiceless living the situation is given the freedom to unfold. You do not grasp one aspect over another for there is nobody to grasp. When you understand something and live it without being stuck to the formulation, what you have understood dissolves in your openness. In this silence change takes place of its own accord, the problem is resolved and duality ends. You are left in your glory where no one has understood and nothing has been understood.

You have said that the only reason objects exist is so as to point to the ultimate perceiver, what we really are. Don't you think that there exist objects which, by their very nature, put us in direct contact with the Ultimate? I was thinking of works of art, for these seem to me to stem directly from the heart of the artist.

When talking of works of art, we must first of all distinguish between true works of art and what we might call artistic works. A work of art always arises from the background: consciousness. Be it music, painting, architecture, poetry or sculpture, it is always seen by the artist in an instant, like a flash of lightning, as it surges forth from deep within him. Afterwards he elaborates it, gives it body and form, in time and space. The Last Supper by Leonardo da Vinci was undoubtedly conceived in perfect simultaneity. We can say the same of the Art of the Fugue by Bach and of certain of Mozart's compositions. An artist worthy of this name is never preoccupied by the material he uses, nor even by the subject matter or the anecdotal side of his work. His only interest is to arrange the different elements in perfect harmony so that they all fuse together and no longer impress the viewer as separate objects. The objective side of his work is thus eliminated. Tagore said that the aim of a true work of art is to give a form to what escapes definition. Then the viewer will no longer be seduced by the material used nor even by the anecdotal content; instead he will be immediately plunged into a non-state which is the aesthetic experience. Later he will qualify the object as beautiful because it stimulated awareness of his own beauty. We can thus see that a work of art is really but a vehicle, a means by which we are led towards the experience. It is truly creative. We feel what the artist himself felt at the time of creation: a spontaneous offering free from all desire for approval.

All objects point to the Ultimate, but the difference between an ordinary object and a work of art is that the ordinary object is passive in its pointing towards the Ultimate whereas the work of art is active.

You said that the object stimulates our own beauty but I thought beauty had no cause...

Apparently a beautiful object stimulates our own beauty because sense perception functions in time and space. But in the moment of living the beauty there is no object nor experiencer present. It is a timeless moment, where you live your fullness. So cause and effect are only on the relative level. They are simply concepts because they cannot be experienced simultaneously. Consciousness is always one with its object. There are never two—always one.

What gives the object this power?

Only a work of art born from beauty, in simultaneity, can point to beauty. Beauty is the same in all. When the artist spontaneously offers his most profound nature and through his talent finds its nearest expression, it awakens in the viewer, the listener, his own profundity. But when you live in beauty and look from beauty, everything points in different ways to your wholeness. Living is no longer from the divided mind. All belongs to your fullness.

But I am not sure everybody is capable of being openly receptive to these works of art.

Before encouraging people to find beauty in a work of art, we must first teach them how to see, how to listen. We will soon realize how difficult this is: listening and seeing are arts in themselves. To arrive at aesthetic experience we must be totally receptive, welcoming, free from memory, so that we are open to the play of color, sounds, rhythms and shapes. This openness, seeing, is the light underlying all sensations and sooner or later, we find ourselves knowingly in this light. Looking at a work of art in this way is truly creative. There is no analysis in it. Each time we are struck by it, it brings us back to our real Self.

As one comes closer to you, at some point or other you encourage your friends to learn to appreciate beauty in art and music and our surroundings. You obviously feel this is a very important "sadhana." How exactly can an appreciation of art help us ask "Who am I?" more effectively?

All our senses, sight, hearing, touch, taste and smell have been channelled or dispersed towards personal defense and aggression, used as tools to maintain the person. Through artistic appreciation the qualities of sensitivity and receptivity are awakened. Energy is sustained and the sense organs find their organic multi-dimensionality. In real listening the ear does not grasp the sound but remains totally relaxed and receptive to sound, silence and rhythm. It becomes a creative tool for the transmission of sound to the whole body. The senses no longer function fractionally but the body is one whole sense organ. Without this welcoming openness, global feeling and sensitivity, the question "Who am I?" remains intellectual. If it is ever to become a living question it must be transposed on every level of our being. The openness in the living question is the doorway to the living answer.

$\mathcal{L}$iberation does not concern the person, for liberation is freedom from the person. Basically the disciple and teacher are identical. Both are the timeless axis of all action and perception. The only difference is that one "knows" himself for what he is while the other does not.

But personality plays a very important part in everyday life, everything depends on it, doesn't it?

The personality is nothing other than a projection, a habit created by memory and nourished by desire. Ask yourself the question "Who am I?" and lucidly observe that the questioner, thinker, doer, sufferer are all forms that appear and disappear within the consciousness of "I am," the ever-living background. They have no reality in themselves. What we call the person is due to a mistake. Thoughts, feelings and actions appear and disappear indefinitely, creating an illusion of continuity. The idea of being a person, an ego, is nothing other than an image held together by memory.

Creativity is an expression of the ultimate but when there is a forgetting of oneself as the ultimate there is insecurity and identification with the created. The world of so-called objects is, like the ego, only a projection. Thinking that you are this or that is only part of your imagination, an hallucination. The teacher helps you to understand, by his unconditional presence and his gift of teaching, that you are neither object nor ego. What you are fundamentally cannot be objectified. It does not refer to time and space.

How can I free myself from mental confusion?

Simply be aware of it. Observe how you function without the slightest idea of changing anything. Vigilance purifies the mind and sooner or later will place you knowingly beyond it.

You encounter ups and downs in your search for the Self because you do not yet see things in their true perspective— as a whole. This instability will continue just as long as you consider yourself as the body and mind. The mind will lead you astray until you perceive its true nature. This insight is the result of listening, free from the past. Live with the sayings of the teacher and the reminders of truth these awaken. These unspoken reminders are the perfume of that to which they refer. Attune yourself to this stillness and not with what you are not. Why identify with the world? All existence is an expression of consciousness. What you are fundamentally is without cause, is completely autonomous, so that taking yourself for an individual doer who lives in a world of choice is an illusion of the ego.

You must turn to this impersonal background as often as the opportunity beckons. Take note that your attention is constantly turned either towards objects or to ideas. A sense of being without qualification is completely unknown to you. Become the spectator, become aware of the natural flow of life, your motives, actions and what results from them. Observe the walls you have built around yourself. As you become more aware of your body and mind you will come to know yourself. As this image of things as you believe them to be subsides, you will have a clear insight of what you are

—something quite other than a product of the mind. You will gradually feel less and less involved in whatever comes up and one day you will discover yourself to be in the perceiving. Once you free yourself from the idea, "I am my body" and the consequences of this idea, you will awaken to your natural state of being. Give yourself up entirely to this discovery. True awareness cannot be obtained by projecting known factors in terms of concepts and perceptions. What you are fundamentally cannot be experienced through reason and is only reached once you eliminate what you are not.

A wilful ego hinders you from being. The witness must enter upon the scene, enabling the ego to be recognized for what it is, an object. This witness is a pedagogical device that opens the door to being. The ego cannot "know" itself because it identifies with what it thinks, feels, experiences. For the ego, there is nothing but resistance, defense, agitation. It is the witness that shines forth and shows up the ego for what it is, an illusion.

The contemplative witnessing state leads us to discover what we are not. We become aware of our body and thought-patterns, the reasons that motivate our actions of which we were previously scarcely conscious. When we observe thought without interference or evaluation, without reference, the thought vanishes in the observing. As the emphasis is no longer on the thought process and content but on the observing itself this witness state becomes a purification, a letting go, without there being a person who purifies or lets go. A whole world of unsuspected energies releases itself. Mental activity ceases to be agitated and spontaneously follows its natural course. We discover ourselves in attention. We completely abandon the "I am this, I am that," reflex. This attention transcends the experience and the experiencer. It is pure awareness.

The world exists only when we think about it; creation stories are for children. In reality the world is created at every moment. It is only memory that gives the false impression of continuity. The individual has no independent existence. It is a fabrication of memory and habit. Always agitated, it hopes and claims, striving to accumulate, searching for confirmation and security. Basically it is frightened and does not dare question itself profoundly.

All perceptions, all experiences are connected with time, are transitory, but our real nature transcends time. It is a lack of clear-sightedness that causes us to identify with temporality. When timeless moments solicit you, accept the invitation. Go deep within it, until you find yourself in your absence.

Once you said: There is only truth. Is not the ego then also truth?

The only truth is being, which is causeless, autonomous. When you see false things for what they are then that is illumination. Renunciation takes place without there being someone who renounces. In this, the direct path, free from choice, there is a freeing of energy and a spontaneous establishment in true being.

The world exists because you exist, but you are not the world. Objects of consciousness, names and forms, are the world. But reality, ever still, is beyond them. It is purely by reflex that you insist upon the name and form, and thus reality escapes you.

There is nothing outside consciousness. The universe, your personal I—all appear within it. The imagination has separated us from this awareness, this consciousness, and we have surrounded ourselves, closed ourselves in with fears, concepts and images. The waking state and dream state are both imposed upon this still awareness which we all have in common.

What you do is of no importance whatsoever; what matters is the way in which you do it, your inner attitude. The role you play on the world's stage has no meaning other than the clear-sightedness with which you play it. Don't lose yourself in your performance-this only blurs the vision of your inner being.

Disinterested action does not bind you but, on the contrary, leaves you entirely free. Live in the moment, simply be. Making a choice depends upon memory and easily becomes slavery. Live as being and you will awaken to bliss.

$\mathcal{W}$e are not the body. But before saying this it seems to me that we must know exactly what the body is that we are not.

The body consists of the five senses. Without these senses we could not talk of a body. We mainly experience it as feeling; we sense it. The sensations that appear to us can be very varied: I feel heavy or light, warm or cold, tense or relaxed. These sensations are memories and habits to which we are accustomed. They are but a means by which the "I am the body" idea reassures itself that it exists. That is to say they are superimpositions on the primal, natural state of the body. So when we say "I must first know what I am not," it means we must be totally aware of these superimpositions.

You talk of feeling the primal state of the body. How can we get to know this primal feeling?

As I said, sensations such as we know them are conditioned feelings which belong to the "I am the body" idea. It is in this superimposition that the person, the I, finds a hold, for the person needs to locate itself either in sensations or in ideas. The only way to become free from conditioning is to look without memory, without the accomplice to the conditioning. Let whatever feelings appear within you come up without visualizing or concentrating on them. In letting the feeling appear before the witness "I," before attention without periphery or center, the body goes through several degrees of elimination, for all superimposition dissolves before this witness. You will observe a letting go of the conditioning. The emphasis that was wrongly put on the conditioning so as to reassure the person, now switches to the observation, to the witnessing, and you will soon find yourself to be the light beyond the witnessed. This is your natural state of total expansion which is energy, vacant and light.

At first the new body sensation will be fragile and you may be solicited by the old patterns. But the body has an organic memory, a memory of its natural state of ease, which, once reawakened and sustained, will sooner or later become permanent. The old sensations will become foreign to you. You may even find it difficult to recall them. Then you will realize that the body appears in you, in awareness, and that you are not lost in the body.

You speak of this new body-sensation as energy. Is this feeling more or less stagnant or does it vibrate?

This new body sensation does not belong to the neuro-muscular system, it is of a much finer nature. It suffuses and radiates in the space around you. This energy is of such a nature that it knows no hindrance, it permeates all that is an obstacle to the physical body, it is beneficial, it is love.

It seems to me that the radiation you are talking about belongs to tactile sensation. What is the experience of the natural state of our other senses, hearing, sight, smell and taste?

When the sense organs are freed from past conditioning they cease grasping, de-contract and are receptive to the newness of every moment. When hearing something take note that you fix the sound. Let it go. There must be no concentration. In this non-directed hearing, this multidimensional hearing, many sounds will be heard in succession. Without your choosing or showing a preference for any particular noise, you may observe that they are eliminated until only one sound remains. If you do not focus on this sound it also dies away and you find yourself in pure listening. In the same way, when all taste is eliminated from the mouth, you arrive at the taste of the mouth itself. But to return to hearing, in the end, it reabsorbs itself completely into pure awareness.

You say these energies are completely free, not bound to the physical structure of the body. Does this mean that with the energy body we can undertake all sorts of movements, movements impossible for the physical body?

The subtle body we are speaking about is completely free from the physical structure of the body. Its energy is completely unconditioned, it belongs to the real body, the energetic body. This energy is capable of burning up all the conditioning buried deep in our nerves and muscles. It purifies the physical body of the conditions and sensations imposed by the "I am the body" idea, by the person who needs to feel himself localized and secured. This person acts through likes and dislikes, through fear, actions which in turn react on the neuro-muscular system creating the vicious circle of conditioning.

When this energy comes to life it is not bound by the physical shape of the body. It is completely free, that means it can take any shape imaginable. It is only through this subtle body that the conditioned movements of the physical body can be freed. Let us consider some asanas, or physical postures. First of all, we carry out the movement exclusively with the subtle body. We must be aware, alert, so that the physical body remains completely vacant, for in the beginning when-ever we move the body structure, memory, habit intervenes causing a reaction on the neuro-muscular plane. So when we do a movement with this fine energetic body, the movement must be completely empty of all habitual reflexes. Only when we feel this vacancy can we introduce our physical body to the movement. But now the physical body moves *within* the expanded body and the movements appear in a new way. It is important not to let the conditioned sensations take over again, but to knowingly sustain the feeling of emptiness. This is the only way we can creatively proceed with the body, oth-erwise we reinforce the conditioning.

Usually this energy does not arise with the same intensity in all parts of the body. Certain parts are particularly gifted in the actualization of this subtle sensation, for example, the palms of the hands or the inside of the mouth. These may well be the first parts of the body to which this subtle energy will appear most intensely. If we give attention to the palm of the hand without representing it or making any sort of effort, if we give the tactile sensation the possibility of springing to life of its own accord, then it will spread throughout our whole body. So first find the starting point and then let the energy flow out from there.

How exactly can this physical approach, and certain diets help us find the impersonal self??

If we take a close look at our body we soon realize that it is overburdened by residues left over from inadequate feeding earlier in life. It creates an impression of density, and dulls our senses, preventing us from feeling our transparency. It is very interesting to observe that, if we give it the right conditions, the body eliminates these residues. With a well adjusted diet of healthy food our whole body begins to react differently and this unquestionably entails changes on the mental and psychological planes. In the same way some forms of body movement can help us become conscious of and locate the parts of the body that are overburdened, solid, dense and congested. They help to free us from fixed ideas of what the body is and enable us to nourish our body with breath. All this is of great value, provided it is carried out with knowledge and great sensitivity. By this I mean that the movements are enacted in awareness, point to that non-objective perspective which is the subject of this talk. All mechanical exercise reinforces the conditioning.

If I let my body and mind follow their natural course without some discipline will they not run away like wild horses?

Letting the movements of your body and mind follow their natural course does not mean passively indulging and identifying with them. This only leads to servitude and misery. You must distinguish between passive letting go and active letting go. In active letting go you remain totally present, clear-sighted, uninvolved and actively alert. Gradually the ego loses its grip until it is reabsorbed into pure awareness. Seeing things no longer from a center is the first step towards permanent freedom, which can only take place if we are free from any form of projection or expectation. If we anticipate, it only disrupts the natural process which must be allowed to come to completion of its own accord. The awareness that shines forth like a flash of lightning in clear-sighted vision cannot possibly take root in a mind which is encumbered.

When you encounter your guru, you must have quite a different approach from the one you usually maintain when you meet people in everyday life where aggressions and defenses are used in pursuit of some goal. At this encounter, you must totally accept yourself, surrender, be ready to receive.

Then your listening will be deeply attentive, completely free from any preconceived ideas. The presence and words of the teacher are the mirror reminding you of, and reflecting, your own open listening, your own presence. Thus the way is shown, the door is opened to grace and you find yourself on the threshold, ready to be taken by your true self.

There are basically two known approaches to truth, the gradual and the direct. In the direct approach the premise is that you *are* the truth, there is nothing to achieve. Every step to achieve something is going away from it. The "path," which strictly speaking is not a path from somewhere to somewhere, is only to welcome, to be open to the truth, the I am. When you have once glimpsed your real nature it solicits you. There is therefore nothing to do, only be attuned to it as often as invited. There is not a single element of volition in this attuning. It is not the mind which attunes to the I am but the I am which absorbs the mind.

In the gradual approach you are bound to the mind. The mind is under the illusion that if it changes, alters states, stops, etc., it will be absorbed in what is beyond it. This misconception leads to the most tragic state in which a truth-seeker can find himself: he has bound himself in his own web, a web of the most subtle duality.

If I am perfect and there is nothing to do, why am I here, why this existence on the planet?

It is only to be knowingly in this perfection. Your use of perfection and imperfection are concepts, interdependent counterparts. The truth that is your nearest fundamental nature is beyond complementarities. In the absence of imperfection and perfection you live in your presence, your wholeness. Be it.

Sir, the answer you have just given to this lady seemed to satisfy her but I don't understand it. Can you come down to my understanding?

You have the capacity of awareness so be aware of those moments when you feel imperfection, a lack, boredom, discontent. When I say, be aware, I don't mean simply name them then go away from them. Rather, give all your attention to the perception. It may take some time because in the beginning you may not be accustomed to looking at yourself. In exploring the boredom or lack you will find you are no longer lost in it, because you will be taken more by the exploration than the object. You will find space within you and the explored. You are no longer stuck in the boredom, the perception, and at a certain moment it suddenly dissolves, and you find yourself in present clarity.

I feel impatient to know the real nature of my existence. Because I still feel no real clarity I am again being taken by objects. Rather than becoming more solicited by silence I am less solicited.

Be alert for those moments when a desire has been fulfilled and an action completed. Be attuned to these moments. They will give freshness to your desire to be. Once the mind is free from anxiety, fear and dissatisfaction, you will see that your only true desire is to be. This desire is completely free from agitation and dispersion. The ardent seeker no longer rushes ahead in his quest for he clearly sees that there is nothing to be found, because nothing was ever lost. It has never ceased to be present. When we clearly see that we are misled by the "searcher," the personality we mistook for ourselves disappears of its own accord. The desire to be comes directly from the Desired—in other words the Self is searching for itself. This insight induces us to abandon our need to accumulate, grasp, accomplish, have, and tends to diminish the mind's activity.

A deep understanding of this brings us spontaneously back to our homeground. Grace draws us to itself. This cannot be described, it can only be lived.

How can I free myself from the continual stream of agitated thoughts?

Simply observe their coming and going. Neither refuse them nor encourage them. In no way direct them. Remain impersonally alert. You will soon feel that thoughts, feelings and sensations appear in this directionless alertness, your openness. They exist only because you are, thus their appearing points to their homeground, the real you. At first you will find that you keep interfering with your thoughts, suppressing or being taken by them. You do this because of the insecurity felt by an ego about to die, an isolated ego. But when you are free from the mental habits of activity and passivity you will find yourself in your natural quiet attention.

So this natural state of attention does not mean I must be completely free from all thoughts?

It is not dependent on the absence of thought. It is that in which thoughts appear and disappear. It is 'behind" thought. So don't be violent or brutal with yourself in the hope of freeing yourself from agitation but be clear-headed. In simple openness which is welcoming you will come to accept and get to know your negative feelings, desires and fears. Once welcomed in non-directed attention these feelings will burn themselves up, leaving only silence. Be alert, ready for each and every appearing and you will soon find yourself the uninvolved spectator of your thoughts. Once this is an established fact, whether thoughts come to mind or not you will not be bound to them.

So if I understand you correctly, when I am invaded by tomorrow's work schedule or family problems or by fantasies, daydreams, I neither indulge them, go with them passively, nor force them away—but simply let the emphasis go from the thought to observing it. Then you say it will dissolve in the observing, is this correct?

Yes.

And once I have felt the non-directed attention do thoughts still come up? Or do they come and go more quickly without becoming a whole story?

They are no longer formulated.

So that there comes a time when the thoughts do not become formulated at all and there is only the impulse to think?

Even the pulsation disappears. There's no longer any fuel for it. It is the subject which maintains the object. When there's no longer a subject the object has no hold. When you are active or passive regarding the coming and going of feelings and thoughts, you see and act from the ego-center but when you come to know the illusory nature of this center you are automatically out of the process. It is the sudden death of all directed energy.

In the observation of thought or subtle impulse there is still a subject/object relationship. It still refers to a center. When you are in awareness there's no more center. Awareness is aware of its surroundings and aware of being aware. The surroundings appear in the awareness. Thus in the end there is no need to go into the meditation laboratory for there is no longer an object, no thought or pulsation.

It seems then that from the state of an agitated mind to the disappearance of the pulsation to think, project, there is a transitional phase. Is this so?

From the very beginning we emphasize the ultimate non-state, the awareness itself. There is no progression from one state or level to another. Thoughts and pulsations appear in this awareness. One cannot progress in meditation. There is no evolution of consciousness. Being observing, the ultimate witness, is an instantaneous occurrence. Experiences and experimentation occur within this natural non-state. In progress there is no progress. Progressions and transitions appear equally in the continuum that never progresses nor regresses.

If there is no progress what is memory?

Memory is a way of thinking. When there is a thought this thought appears in the now. We label it 2000 years ago or yesterday but the label is also a present thought. There's only one function at a given time so that at the moment of functioning you are one with the functioning.

If I am one with the functioning and nothing is outside it how can it be remembered later in time?

The fact that it is remembered proves that it appeared in your global awareness. This is what we mean by saying consciousness and its object are one. It is also sometimes called witnessing. In this global awareness things appear from so-called past or future but they all belong to the universal present. In reality therefore there is no memory. It is function in awareness, in witnessing.

When do we witness our actions?

You are always witnessing your actions, so don't try to witness. Witnessing is not a function and cannot be represented. It is extremely important that you realize that you are the witness and that you cannot try to be it. It is enough that you become fully aware that you are the witness, for that eliminates the old patterns and the habit you have of considering yourself to be the thinker or doer.

When you act you are one with the action, it is only afterwards that the ego appropriates the act from which it was absent, and says "I have done this." At the moment of acting there is only acting, without an actor.

Once the interfering subject is recognized as nonexistent it disappears. What remains is pure consciousness. Without the egosubject there can be no subject/object relation so that what appeared to be an object can no longer rightly speaking be one. It is nothing but an expression of this reality, this stillness.

Should we not make some effort to improve ourselves?

What do you want to improve? You are perfect; uncover the person who feels something is missing, and what remains is perfection. What is false disappears of its own accord, once it has been seen as false. You identify yourself with your body and your mind and because of this you want to improve. You will be dominated by these instruments just as long as you believe in them.

The moment you no longer believe you are the body and mind the energy used up in this error will be freed. Leave the mind and body free to be what they are and you will no longer be their slave. They are only fragments of the whole which you are. Simply take note of your imperfections and this awareness will take care of them. Once you understand that you are not the body and the mind, you can then accept whatever happens. Understanding your fundamental autonomy brings you to an attitude of total acceptance.

Every single thing is seen in the light of this welcoming, appears and disappears within it. As a result, things attain their full significance and harmony reestablishes itself. This welcoming is an alert awareness, uninhabited by the past. It allows whatever presents itself to unfold in and point to the welcoming, without being limited by the ego or deformed by memory.

In this Oneness we discover our nature: ultimate joy, and perfection.

*T*here are moments in daily life when the mind is not agitated. These are windows where Truth can flow in. We should become aware of these moments. They do not come about by will or discipline, rather the outer circumstances bring the mind to quietness. Once the mind stops trying to grasp, once there is no effort to attain and become something, once energy is no longer projected in strategy and end-gaining it returns to a state of equilibrium where everything remains peaceful and points towards silent awareness, within which all thoughts and perceptions come and go.

But cannot we bring about the tranquility of the mind through meditation?

This quiet mind of which I am speaking is not the absence of thought. The absence of thought is a state produced artificially but the mind free from agitation has its own rhythm, its own pulsation. Between these pulsations are gaps of which one must be aware. They are not an absence or a blank state. They are full, presence. Allow yourself to be taken by them.

Truth cannot be perceived. It can only be lived in the non-dual continuum, the non-state where there is neither seer nor seen.

But certain forms of meditation bring one to the quiet mind and prepare one to be taken by what is behind the mantra.

Pronouncing a mantra correctly is a high art rarely achieved. When correctly pronounced it has the power to quiet the mind. When all formulation of the mantra is dissolved through the sound vibration you are one with the perception, the vibration. This vibration is still an object of observation but as you know from your guru that what you are is the light behind all perceptions, even this most subtle object dissolves in your being aware.

The art of the mantra is magic and to learn it takes a very long time and a very talented teacher. Usually you die before you master it!

Can we come to freedom and peace through helping others as Christianity teaches?

If you want to help others, you must be completely free from any need for help. When you experience this you are the biggest help possible to all those surrounding you. It is in non-action that all action is accomplished. You are not the doer of your acts, you are the awareness from which action stems. In relationships between personalities, between objects, there is only looking for security, there's only asking. Even so-called giving is with a view to getting. Pure giving is your true nature, it is love. When the occasion asks you for help you will spontaneously help, and the help coming from wholeness, from love, will be highly effective. But when you are a professional helper acting on an idea you have of yourself or the world your help will always remain fractional.

But before I am realized isn't fractional help better than no help at all?

The idea of helping is anticipation. It is action which comes out of reaction. See the deep motive of your desire to help. Real helping, as I said, comes out of non-action. When the world asks for help, help of course, help with discrimination but don't be a helper.

What do you mean, "help with discrimination"?

Give to your fellow what he needs to accomplish what life asks of *him*. Do not impose on another your idea of how he should best live. Indiscriminate "help" is all around us. It doesn't come out of freedom from the person. In a way such interference is violence, war.

Why do you say that perceiving is closer to truth than a concept?

A perception is the first message given by the senses before the brain names it or the psychological mind qualifies it. Most people's perception of their bodies is atrophied because they go away from the perception and immediately conceptualize it. The perception is always in the present, immediate, but conceptualization is memory. Most of the time we feel and function through memory.

In everyday life we rarely give sensations time to make themselves felt. We prematurely intervene, conceptualizing and qualifying them. Perceptions and concepts cannot exist simultaneously and we tend to cut the perception short before it has fully flourished.

So, if I understand, the senses are in contact with our surroundings but we miss this contact because we live in the memory of former sensation?

Yes, we have conceptualized sensation, crystallized it,

qualified it. Perception, that is cognition, and naming, re-cognition, are natural functions which happen spontaneously without the need for a center of reference, an I, a propagator of opinion. But we go away from these immediate functions, we don't wait for the unfolding of the perception, we don't welcome what our surroundings offer us. When we live in memory we cut ourselves off from the universe, we live in isolation. This is the root of all suffering.

Is perception non-dual or can we move nearer to non-duality?

Perception itself is non-dual, it is one with the awareness within which it appears.

How can we become aware of the awareness in which perception appears?

Pure perception is contained by what we call awareness. In this instance the container and the contents are identical. He who knows the contents, in other words, he who is aware, who "knows" himself as awareness and not as the psyche, is knowingly aware, is present at the time of perceiving. He is the living witness, at the same time the audience and the actor. Once this perception comes to an end, or between two thoughts, he is aware of being, but there is no sensation linked to it.

The background is like a white sheet on which we draw: lines appear, the drawing takes form yet the white sheet does not disappear into thin air. The drawing covers, camouflages the whiteness but the whiteness is still there behind it. Sensa-tions camouflage just like the drawing, so he who does not know himself, "he who is not aware," only sees the discon-tinuous lines, separate one from another, he does not see the white sheet. He is lost in the sensation, forgets himself.

Isn't this awareness of oneself also a perception?

No, it is vital that you understand that awareness can never become an object; it is neither outside nor inside, it is free from time and space. It is the vastness, the container, in which all states, all objects appear. It is your nearest and can never be perceived as the eye cannot see its seeing. The ultimate knower knows itself by itself. It needs no agent to be known. Awareness is not a perception. It is an apperception.

What is the difference between this apperception and what you call direct perception?

Perception calls for a subject/object relation. Direct perception does not go through the mind. It is the same as apperception.

Why can there not be a regression ad infinitum of perceivers?

Consciousness is our totality, our total expression is in consciousness. If consciousness could be perceived it would not be our totality.

Why must we have a totality? Cannot our being be an infinite regression?

If we do not live our totality we live in fraction, in subject/object relationship, in discontinuity. This brings conflict in our life. First accept this state of all appearings, the discontinuity of existence. In real acceptance, the accepted is in the accepting. This accepting is your wholeness. But it must not remain a concept, second-hand information. It must be lived, made first-hand.

Do we have very few pure perceptions?

Yes, very few indeed when you consider that a sort of memory-bank intervenes very frequently. When a perception is pure, there is no memory. For example, I can direct my attention towards the flower and think that I feel it but I do not really feel it, I have only provoked memory. If, on the other hand, I could remain present to the flower and not refer to the past, to memory, the flower would appear as much more than I have stored in my memory. It would surpass all expectation, appearing in its fullness before my innocent eye.

Is this remaining present without letting memory intervene what you mean by listening?

Yes. Listening has no center, it is multi-dimensional welcoming.

You say we cannot go and meditate. What you call meditation is the background, the container, but is not sitting and listening, remaining present, what we would normally call meditation?

This sitting is a laboratory for exploring the motive to want to meditate, for finding the entity who is looking for god, peace, happiness. As long as you have not discovered the nature of the meditator you will continue to sit and look for it. But eventually you will see that the meditator can never find peace, god or happiness because it belongs to the mind, to the intellect. When this is seen, and it happens suddenly, there is no dynamism "to meditate:' All that remains is presence where no one is present to anything.

So should I sit regularly until I find the meditator, or find that it cannot be found?

You can find this at every moment in life. Don't make sitting a practice, a habit, an addiction. Wait until you feel the invitation to simply be quiet.

What shall I do if the invitation doesn't come very often? I have a busy life and it seems to camouflage the invitations.

See that you are lost in your activities. As soon as you see this there is some space between you and your activities.

But I know I am lost in my activities. I am very aware of this fact, that is why I came here and asked you the question. Seeing it is not enough.

You have conceptualized your seeing, because you live in concepts. You have made a thought of being lost and being busy. By seeing I don't mean see intellectually; real seeing is direct perception as we discussed earlier. It is facing the facts, the sensation, the state of things without a justifier, controller, without rationalizing or thinking about them. There is no seer in seeing. It is an instantaneous apperception that occurs when you no longer try to escape the facts. Then all activities are in you but you are not in them. You will no longer feel lost in activities, no longer feel identified with them. On the contrary activities are lost in you.

When meditating, my respiration occasionally troubles me; I feel it as something solid that I would like to stop.

One should neither want to breathe or want to stop breathing. There must not be any volition. Simply watch the coming and going of the breath as you watch a cloud or a bird. You will see that your breathing is full of tension. In letting it simply function your breath will come to its natural organic movement. What is important is that you come to that moment when you feel yourself in being aware. Being aware is listening, listening to whatever presents itself, just as when many different sounds occur, a child playing, a car engine running, a bird singing in a tree, and you don't choose among these sounds nor grasp them. You neither try to ignore them nor pay attention. In this way what you hear is not able to take a hold in you and the energy usually deployed in grasping, in controlling the breath or sound heard, will return back upon itself, and you will experience true listening.

Isn't this listening a perception?

No, it is not a perception. Although this reality knows itself, it is not a subject/object knowing. Listening, non-directed attention, is the natural, the inbuilt, functioning of the brain.

So is listening the same as consciousness or is it an expression of consciousness?

Listening is of the same nature as consciousness. Unconditioned listening is the most subtle function. When listening is sustained it unfolds in consciousness.

How can we be this consciousness, this silence, and at the same time carry out an activity calling for memory, the handling of concepts and other forms of attention?

All of our everyday activities find their full meaning and fulfill all their possibilities in self-knowledge, in this consciousness. Once you are knowingly this awareness, you no longer identify with the mind. Then you will experience a dynamic energy whatever activity you undertake, but it will no longer be a driving force dominated by will, binding you to an object. It too is an expression of consciousness.

What does self-knowledge taste like, feel like? I assume it is not completely flavourless!

The Self knows itself, of its own accord, without the intervention of any means. It cannot be described because it is not in the realm of comparison or complementarity. You cannot smell incense burning nor see the leaf of a plant without using the corresponding sensory organ, but consciousness knows itself all the while the varied aspects of manifestation occur. Water is not altered by the many different fish swimming in its depths, it is ever water. I can give you another analogy. You only taste the things that are in your mouth, the objects, but the mouth has its own taste.

Maybe you cannot fully understand the true vision of things because you are not yet fully convinced that nothing exists on its own outside you, everything finds its being within you. What you see and do are creations of the moment. It is only memory that creates the illusion of continuity. It is memory that proclaims that you were here yesterday or the day before.

So we could say that this knowledge is honey and that we taste it at the same time?

Knowing knows only itself. It is aware of the surroundings and at the same time aware of being aware.

My biggest stumbling block is the world of difference that exists between the intuition I encounter while meditating and the fact that everything is forgotten once I undertake my daily activities. In the end I begin to wonder why I meditate at all, for an hour later I have forgotten everything and am once again submerged by objects.

The problem is this: during meditation you experience and

contemplate a vacant state of mind, what you perceive is the absence of activity. You know this absence but do not yet know the knower. Once you are knowingly this knower, you will be the knowing, whether the mind is active or passive. There will be no difference, no change. From then on this awareness will be unwavering certainty.

The total emptiness which you will experience during meditation is in a way still an object. Absence of thought inevitably implies its eventual complement, presence of thought. Thus although you sense a state of deep peace free from activity, it is very important not to emphasize this blank state, the empty mind. Living meditation is not the absence of mind activity but is the "support" of activity and non-activity. If you emphasize the knower of the empty mind and not the empty mind itself one day this void, this blank, will also vanish and you will encounter ultimate stillness. This stillness will remain during all activities.

Up till now you have contemplated a calmed mind, but should a bird sing or someone speak, your inner silence is broken. That is why you ask this question. By its very nature the mind is occasionally empty; it is nonetheless nothing but an instrument.

What should we do when there is a striving towards something during meditation?

You must simply observe it. Soon attention will shift to this observing and not the object you observe. You will *be* attention, attention without object. This might seem to be a meaningless way to talk about attention because we are accustomed to being attentive towards something. But pure attention is absolutely empty of all direction. It is not focused on an object, it is free of any memory. It is simply expanded alertness.

You spoke of sound. Once there is no more emphasis on it do we still hear it?

As long as the child is crying you still hear it because the function of the ear is hearing. When there is no more emphasis on the sound, that is, when you no longer direct your attention to it, choose it, and name it, then what remains? The inbuilt function continues, it is vibration. The specific sound dies away completely and what remains is pure listening.

Is this not a withdrawal of the senses?

Not at all. Withdrawal is a wilful process and calls for deep concentration. Withdrawal is still looking for a result and maintains the subject/object duality on a subtle level. You can never come to unconditioned listening through withdrawal.

Through withdrawal you can of course eliminate the vibration, the natural function of the senses. It is a kind of *samadhi*, an experience you enter and leave. But why pursue such experiences? They have nothing to do with *sahaja*.

The word meditation has been misused by many traditions which have adopted so many techniques.

Is the consciousness within which manifestation takes place one?

From this point of view one cannot say you and I. "You" and "I" as body and mind appear and disappear each with their own qualities, but they are nothing other than a collection of memories which have no existence in themselves. Just as waves and foam are nothing but sea, as separate entities they have only a temporary existence.

Can't we attribute these memories to the person?

As long as you take yourself to be "a wave" or "the foam" you cannot see this truth. All I ask is that you cease to identify yourself with them. You will then know your real essence: "the sea."

But this does not prevent us from seeing the waves, can we see them and still know that we are the sea?

It is only when one sees things from the standpoint of the sea that one can talk of waves and foam, for then they are truly waves and foam. They do not have a separate entity, they are no longer isolated projections of memory. They gain their true significance and true relation as expressions of wholeness.

In everyday life don't we need memory?

No, the situation always provides the adequate attitude, not memory. You are the owner of all memories but you are not the memories. You must realize that you are now only a heap of conventions, habits, what society has made of you. Once all these have left you, you will realize that they were defenses and aggressions accumulated solely to maintain this ego which simply does not exist. Then the real Self shines forth. It does not belong to memory. It is there because it is there. See this! Listen! You are not this memory. Get to know those moments when you are nothing, you will feel such freedom! Then all is possible.

Between memory and freedom is there an in-between state?

No, there is no half way. In the silence we are talking about, we are unconditionally free. In this silence we are strictly nothing. Memory intervenes only when we believe ourselves to be someone. When we are nothing, everything is possible. This freedom has its own unique taste; it is not the result of a political or social point of view but on the contrary engenders it. As long as this experience is not lived there is no freedom, be it political or social; there is only dictatorship.

Is there any difference between this freedom and grace?

Freedom is grace and grace is this freedom.

Is this grace permanent?

Grace has always been and always is, waiting to be welcomed. When grace is established we can no longer speak of grace, otherwise it remains a concept. We can only say it is truly living in the moment. In this is joy, total security without cause because this living in the timeless moment is causeless.

But it is pure torture to have heard of this without living it!

Your idea of torture is the only obstacle preventing you from living it.

When I transform this experience into a concept, when I objectify it, I leave truth behind to return to the turmoil of life. It is incomprehensible to me that it might happen yet I have a feeling it is so.

It is in the nature of truth to express itself as an object, but since the object arises from truth, the seeker intuitively retains knowledge of its origin. Knowing that, the seeker is no longer dispersed but centered on truth and the foretaste of reality is very strong. This insight brings about a letting-go, a retracing of one's steps that leads you to pure consciousness, to your effortless being.

$\mathcal{H}$e who longs to know his true nature must first understand his mistaken identification with objects: "I am this," "I am that." All identifications, all states are transitory and consequently unreal. Identifying the "I" with this or that is the root of ignorance. Ask yourself what is permanent throughout all the stages of life. The question "Who am I?" will be found to have no answer. You cannot experience what is permanent in a subject/object relationship, as something perceivable. You can only formulate and explain that which you are not. What you fundamentally and continually are cannot be put into words or reasoned out. Being is non-dual, absolute and constant, ever present whatever the circumstances.

When we consider the knower independently of the known, he reveals himself to be pure witness. When knowledge and the knower are one, there is no longer a place for a witness.

All imagination is unreal, based on memory. But all that is not anticipated, all that is unexpected, that causes wonder, astonishment, surges forth from living reality. The quest for pleasure, for satisfaction, is born of suffering, of memory. Welcome life as it comes; don't emphasize the world but change your attitude towards it. Your idea of the world, of society, stems from the belief that you are a separate ego. Be your totality and the world will change. The world is not other than you. The world is in you; society begins with you.

You say we should not begin by trying to change the world but we can change our attitude towards it. Is this what you mean when you say that existence is the film but we are not the film, we are the light illuminating the film?

Yes. You cannot change the film because all attempts to change it belong to the film.

Identification with your body and your personality binds you, making you dependent. Our sensorial perceptions are built up by memory and imply a knower. We must closely examine the nature of the knower. This requires all our attention, all our love. Thus you will discover what you really are. That is the only sadhana. To integrate awareness of the Self is freedom. The Self takes charge of everything.

Images arise and fade away in the mirror of consciousness, and memory creates the illusion of a continuity. Memory is but a mode of thinking, it is purely transitory. On such an unsteady basis we construct a whole world of characters. This illusion hinders clear seeing.

Striving to improve or to progress only confuses us even more. Outward appearances may lead us into believing we have reached a state of stability, that changes are taking place, that we are progressing and are on the threshold of grace. But in fact nothing has changed. We have merely rearranged our furniture. All this activity takes place in the mind, it is a figment of imagination.

It is all much more simple than that. Why make it so complicated? What you fundamentally are is always here, always complete. It needs no purification. It never changes. For the Self there is no darkness. You cannot discover or become truth for you are it. There is nothing to do to bring it closer, nothing to be learned. See only that you are constantly trying to go away from what you are. Stop wasting time and energy in projecting. Live this stopping, not lazily and passively, but live the alertness that is found in the stopping of expectation and anticipation. This also is your sadhana.

There is no room for improvement in reality. It is perfection itself. How could you possibly get nearer to it? There is no means by which you can approach it.

Is it not fatalistic to say we cannot change the film?

Fatalistic means you identify with the film and submit to it. In fact, the film goes on but you are the seer. Being off the screen will give you a new outlook on what the film really is. From this global, infinite view, which is no longer a viewpoint, which is not in time or space, everything happens in perfect simultaneity. So there is nothing to change.

Going back to our earlier conversation, you said the world changes when my perception of it changes. How can this be?

One who has reached full maturity, who knows himself in consciousness will not necessarily conform with social convention. Such a one will act at the right moment as the situation dictates, without anybody being hindered in any way. If your acts are dictated by your desires, you have no freedom whatsoever. On the other hand, if you do what the situation calls for, you do what is right and you and your surroundings are free.

The sage has not the slightest idea of being a person when he acts, feels, thinks. The ego is totally absent. The ego itself is no more than a thought and two thoughts cannot take form simultaneously so identification with the ego only takes place once the thought concerning the object has subsided. Then it claims this thought as its own. The sense of ownership, "I saw it, I did it," comes after the fact and has nothing to do with the fact. Once this mechanism becomes clear, you realize that the identification you previously took to be real is but an illusion. You neither own nor are a slave to the situation. Your true nature transcends it. Silent awareness is not a state but is the continuum in which all states, all things appear and disappear. The words we use in the waking state to talk about the non-state are an expression of this awareness. When we live in awareness all is an expression of awareness.

The world you perceive is none other than a figment of the imagination founded on memory, fear, anxiety and desire. You have locked yourself away within this world. See this without jumping to conclusions and you will be free. There is no need whatsoever for you to free yourself from a world which exists only in your imagination.

What you take to be reality is only a concept arising from memory. Memory arises from the mind, the mind from the witness, the witness from the Self. You are the witness, the onlooker standing on the bank watching the river flow on. You do not move, you are changeless, beyond the limits of space and time. You cannot perceive what is permanent, because you are it.

Do not nourish the ideas you have built around yourself nor the image people have of you. Be neither someone nor something, just remain free from the demands of society. Don't play its game. This will establish you in your autonomy.

The example, so often mentioned by Vedanta, of the snake and the piece of rope, refers to the world on one hand and ultimate reality on the other. The snake represents the world of objects where we find persons, thoughts and affectivity; the rope represents ultimate reality, silent awareness. Once we cease to take the rope for a snake, the idea of the snake fades away and we see the rope for what it really is. It is perfectly natural that errors lose their substance and vanish when truth becomes evident. Since thought is an integral part of the illusion, it cannot possibly reveal ultimate reality to us. "Isness," presence, which is the source of all experience, is beyond the experiencer/experienced duality. When the accent is on being aware, and not on thought nor on perception, we gradually become deeply relaxed, both on the neuro-muscular level and on the mental plane.

If we disinterestedly observe the arising and disappearing of all the states we experience, we soon come to realize that each state, each perception, each thought, is reabsorbed into an unspoken knowing, knowing as being. This, the continuum, the only reality, is there before activity commences. Let yourself sink deep within this stillness each time it makes itself felt.

You cannot expect reality to appear, for it ever is. Events appear and disappear. Never forget the passing character of all experience, this is all you need to do and the door to grace will open before you. As soon as opinions and reactions such as "I like, I don't like" intervene, you have fallen into the personal habit and you weave a web around yourself and lose sight of your true nature. Feelings of antipathy and sympathy lead you to turn your back on the Self. Your ideas of change, progress, better and worse are fractional and personal. When you look at the world from wholeness the world will change in you. You are the world.

Is the freedom from thought I experience in meditation close to my real nature? Is it the same stillness you talk about?

In what is habitually called meditation, you strive to rid yourself of all intentions and concepts. Thus you find yourself before a screen free of thoughts, be they objective or subjective. Having rid yourself of these thoughts others, more rebellious, appear, invade you indiscriminately and you again eliminate them. It is true that after practicing this for a certain length of time, mental activity lessens. However, if the seeker is not guided by an authentic teacher this empty screen will always remain a mystery. The silent awareness we are talking about is beyond the absence or presence of thoughts, words, activity or passivity. These arise from and are reabsorbed into stillness beyond the mind, stillness beyond freedom from thought. Nothing whatsoever can affect this tranquility. Objective knowledge is perceived by means of the corresponding organ in the body, but silent awareness does not require a means.

Are conflict and war inevitable attributes of the human being?

Conflict is an attribute of the individual, not the human being. In your real nature which is oneness no conflict is possible. Effort, competition and aggression only concern the person. Ask yourself just how enslaved you are to your opinions and habits which are the source of perpetual conflict. Observe how your mind works, look at how it functions, look without any preconceived ideas. A moment will come when you discover yourself in the looking, not in the mind. Subsequently, when all striving has dissolved, you will realize that you are the light shining beyond even the observer. Reality is neither a product of the mind nor the result of a whole train of thoughts, it just is. You must realize that you can never find your true self in a perception. The only method we can suggest is to observe without analysis the way in which your mind reacts in the different circumstances of everyday life. Don't alter your life to fit some idea. Live as previously, thinking and feeling, only become aware of these as simply functions, thus you will become spontaneously free from them. Then what you think of as your personality will vanish, leaving only the witness. In the end, even this will lose itself in ultimate knowledge.

That which surges forth unexpectedly, on the spur of the moment, without any cause, free from the past; that which springs forth without roots and neither flowers nor fades; that which is most natural, free from strain, is the Self.

The living "I know," being the knowing, completely escapes memory. You can only remember what you have actually understood on a mental plane at a given time, that is, an experience. But life itself is not bound to time and space, it is not experience, not objectifiable. Living entirely detached from the mind's hold is nondual, pure being. The real teacher who knows life is beyond what he teaches. Knowing the Self, being knowledge, cannot be communicated by words alone. Words are but a very pale reflection of the inexplicable Self, and communication by words must never become a limitation. The teaching is only a "pretext" to bring the disciple to a new quality of listening, a listening that is totally open, receptive and free from any concept or anticipation. This openness is the listener's own true nature: stillness, ultimate knowledge. The teaching should never give a hold to any physical or psychological fixation. When the teacher is free from being a teacher, though the teaching is in space and time, it unwaveringly points towards true being, the domain in which the teaching originates. The so-called teacher helps the so-called disciple free himself from the patterns of body and mind, allowing him to find his real autonomy and ultimate security, the continual non-state.

Learning things objectively is always a fragmentary process. The guru passes on the knowledge of truth in its totality, for he and his teachings are one. Simply by his or her presence the teacher helps because this presence reminds the seeker of his own presence which he is in common with the teacher and in which all existence appears. Unintentional reminders of totality thus will come about and the disciple will be attracted by them. What was knowingly lived in the teacher's presence will renew itself. The permanent establishing in reality is instantaneous; the reorchestration of the energy of the body-mind is a question of time.

If I understand correctly, the guru's teaching points towards our true Self and by so doing leaves us with frequent reminders of what took place in his presence. Words are only a stepping stone and they will soon die out revealing silence free from objects, plenitude, the Self.

Quite right.

What is the correct way to listen to the guru when he talks of the spiritual perspective?

The disciple must totally accept all the teacher communicates to him; this implies that he be completely free of any preconceived idea, way of thinking or belief. He is totally open-minded. While the teaching takes place his inner nature will make itself felt, since what he is *not* becomes more and more clear and is eliminated.

What is the chief obstacle preventing fulfilment?

The chief obstacle to the fulfilment of our potential is the concept of a me. It is nothing but a figment of the imagination created by memory and by the social context we find ourselves in.

It is a fact that once a desired object has been acquired,

there is a brief moment of desirelessness, a moment free from all intention, from the me, the knower and the known. It is only later that the *me* stakes a claim to this experience and transforms it into "I am happy," into a subject/object relationship. The me is never present but is made of memory and thus uses memory to exist. So although there is no me at the time of the experience, no subject/object relation, memory ascribes the cause of this wonderment, desirelessness, to an object, thus reinforcing the whole process that makes us seek fulfillment in objects.

But if the ego habitually destroys oneness where does the desire for fulfillment, desirelessness, come from?

If the ego is in the slightest way separated from its source, it yearns to find it again. This search comes from the remembrance of unity and plenitude. As every experience emanates from the non-experience which is our real being, the me also bears the scent of its source. This remembering is awakened through those moments of desirelessness and in deep sleep. The ego is thus in permanent conflict, at once longing for its own oblivion in oneness and at the same time habitually fighting for its very existence.

Recalling the object as being the cause of wonderment reinforces the subject/object relation of which the me is king. Understanding that the object is only a pointer to the objectless displaces the stress put on it. This produces an intimate awakening, a forefeeling of wholeness, which, together with the ego, dissolves, spontaneously revealing the Self.

How can we get rid of the idea of the ego?

Within us there is the deep-rooted belief-system, based on illusion, that all objects and our surroundings are separate from us, outside us. Yet we identify with the body, senses and mind and create a separate world of I and you. In the beginning it is very helpful to take our belief to its full extension and see our feelings, body, thoughts and so on as objects just like others, like a tree, a horse, a bird. This gives some space in the irrational, tight relation we have with the body-mind. We come to see that our thoughts, the I-thought, emotions, likes and dislikes are equally all perceivable objects. This standpoint leads us to realize spontaneously that we are the knower, and the notion of being a personal entity loses all meaning.

The conception of our surroundings as a mass of objects will be transmuted. The object is no longer truly speaking an object; from now on it is an extension, an expression of the knower, consciousness. This is the result of total understanding, grasped in an instant. This experience is of quite a different nature from the analytical process which proceeds step by step.

Can this understanding arise at any moment?

This flash of understanding can occur at any time whether in the waking state, in the dreaming state, or when passing from deep sleep to the waking state. It and it alone causes all set patterns to vanish and to reintegrate in the whole.

For most people, attention is only understandable as concentration directed towards something, or as deriving from the attraction of an object. The stress we put on the object that interests us creates the illusion of a continuity. Non-directed attention enables the object to melt into silent stillness, the ultimate non-dual consciousness, which is the background of all apparent duality.

Total understanding is instantaneous, leaving no room whatsoever for a question or interpretation. In this flash of clear sightedness space and time are abolished. Choosing between long and short, good and evil, is a conceptual process, due to our identification with the material side of things, the body. Understanding is of a different nature, it rises above opposition and complementarity. Only this total knowledge can dissolve all conditioning.

When talking of spiritual matters, what is your idea of God?

It is a concept.

What is a concept?

An idea or a thought.

And what is a thought?

An image evoked by visual, auditory or tactile memory, an object.

Are all thoughts objects?

Yes, except the thought "I am," which has no material substance and arises directly from non-objectifiable living.

How can I come to this experience?

It is beyond space and time and cannot be experienced.

Can you talk more about this so that I might eventually understand it?

Go away from beliefs, ideas and concepts to what is closest to you, your physical and psychological state at this moment.

Your surroundings start with your body, your vitality. Whatever should present itself on the spur of the moment must be accepted as a whole (accepted means free from will, we are not talking here of the opposing terms of acceptance and refusal). Condemning or refusing will not set you free; on the contrary, it only weighs you down, imprisons you. You can only see facts when there is nobody choosing, and only through the facts can you find total freedom.

When you listen without being aggressive or resisting, your whole body becomes this listening, it is not confined to the ears. Everything surrounding you is included in this global listening, and ultimately there is no longer a listener and something listened to. You are then on the threshold of non-duality. You have left conceptual patterns behind. Don't just talk about it, live it for yourself.

If I have well understood, living is what is left when all thought has come to an end, when all sensations have subsided.

You have preconceived patterns of thinking. Living is an absolutely non-objectifiable continuum, an ever present now. All thought, feeling and sensation spring spontaneously from this living. Consciousness does not depend on the absence of thought or sensation. Do not emphasize the absence of objects. Emphasize only the presence of consciousness, life. Consciousness is in the absence and presence of thought and sensation.

In this case what are the world and objects surrounding us?

When the body wakes up in the morning the world appears. It is perceived by the five senses and conceived by the sixth sense, the brain. There are infinite forms and names but they have no existence outside of consciousness. To paraphrase the Zen saying: First there are conceptual mountains, then there are no concepts, then there are perceptual mountains.

Is there any meaning in the relationship between the I and the world?

There is no aim. God is perfection and beyond improvement. If we want to talk in terms of an aim, the world and objects are there only to reveal the ultimate subject, "I am."

Is God the same as consciousness for you? Is our natural being God?

Yes, there are not two. In our absence as somebody there is God. This absence belongs also to God. There is only God.

$\mathcal{W}$e meet here all together, but in reality we meet only ourselves. In a meeting of personalities there is only demanding, asking, the desire to overcome the feeling of isolation and insecurity that the ego finds itself in all the time. So-called love and giving between personalities, between objects, still arises out of insecurity and the need for security. Real contact is made once there is no person to be met, in a place which cannot be located in time and space.

We exchange ideas so as to know their worth, to find the most correct way of seeing things, but under no circumstances do we try to situate ourselves in relation to a thought or a projection. Basically it is a form of higher reasoning which is meant to bring about its own elimination, so that sooner or later you will find there is no room for personal identity. Then, everything that preceded the living knowing is totally eliminated. There remains only a deep inner peace free from conflict and problems, where nothing needs to be added or subtracted. In this oneness there is no difference whatsoever between you and me. But your present situation is that you know your thoughts, your emotions and feelings, but you don't know the knower. This is the only difference between us now.

The answer given by one who knows himself to be, never derives from memory. Each and every real answer flows directly from this being knowledge. Welcome the answer with awakened attention, and then forget it. It is indispensable that we let go of the spoken word so that the essence behind it may spring to life within the questioner. When contemplating the sayings of the guru you recall them, not so much from the mind but from the Truth from which they spring. It is not the verbal syntax that has transformative power but the source from which the words come, and with which they are impregnated. It is the feeling of the source which brings the words back to you.

Is it like when you are far from your beloved and you have the urge to be with her and there's a strong desire to be alone, go for a walk in a quiet place, getaway from the activity of daily life? You have the strong desire to be absorbed in love.

That is perfect as long as you don't fix yourself in the physical presence.

But is it not important to understand the words with the intellect?

If you sustain mental activity, if you try to understand on the mental plane, the true answer cannot find you. It is only when the mind dissolves that the true answer comes to life. Trying to evaluate the words in terms of what you know only keeps you in the question. We must very carefully distinguish between questions rooted in memory, in the past, and those which spring up in the moment itself free from second-hand information. These creative questions already contain the seeds of the answer. When we ask the question we do not yet know the answer, but we intuitively feel it to be very near at hand.

It seems that for many of us here the words are still not clear. I see people sitting around you with a smile on their faces who have no questions. Where are they?

They are engulfed in affectivity, in states, and feel themselves in the donkey-stall. Certain people need to be in the stall in order to know the way out. One day they will see this state objectively and know that they, the seer, are out of it. It is the same process for intellectuals who are enclosed in concepts and ideas. At the moment of seeing the situation clearly they know that the seer is out of this cage.

Understanding must be clearly articulated in the intellect. A clear intellect frees you from the hold of states and projection. At a certain point the intellect spontaneously gives itself up to being the knowing, and you find yourself in your equanimity.

You say that in formulating questions and listening to answers we must not analyze, evaluate or interpret. I feel this denies the natural intellect and brings about a state of passive not-inquiring. What exactly is the function of the intellect in asking and listening?

In listening the answer goes through the intellect but you are not stuck to it. The saying goes at once to being understanding. The intellect must understand the words, the symbols, and come to a kind of clear geometrical representation of that to which they point. But at the same time the intellect knows its limits, that it is limited by representation, and then the representation dissolves and only the essence remains. Let's make it clearer: If I say "pear" you cannot think of it without representing it either mentally or sensorially. But if we talk of "deep peace" or "unconditioned love" you spontaneously leave the representation and come to a feeling which dissolves all concepts. The teacher uses words only to help the student come to this dissolving of concepts so that what is left is only peace or love.

So no matter what the question is, the teacher always brings us back in one way or another to non-representation?

Yes. The teacher can remain silent in certain circumstances. The silence, beingness, gives no hold for representation, for being this or that. The words used point beyond the mind, senses and feeling. You know how different words strike you: table, fork or bag remain simply in representation, but wife, lover, child, stepfather, war, death, my country, all have a strong emotional impact. The words of the guru go neither in the representational nor psychological network, and should never be kept on these levels. It is only in their dissolving in listening that they can be effective.

So if one does not understand your words or forgets them, there can still be some benefit?

When you neither try to remember nor forget, when you are free from all personal relation with the words, they can be effective. The perfume of the words will come back to you at some point. Don't try to remember, only let yourself be remembered.

And if I don't understand what you are saying?

When you say "I understand" you haven't understood, all you have done is interpret the words according to your intellectual framework and capacities. Understanding does not come on the mental level.

This does not mean the intellect should be sleepy or passive. On the contrary, a clear mind is essential so that you do not fall into emotional and psychological states.

The thing that bothers me and that I see as the Catch-22 of teachers

in the spiritual path is that they are by definition self-referential.
Anything that appears as incorrect teaching or behavior is explained
away as lack of insight on the part of the disciple. In this way many
false prophets hold a vast audience. How can we come to know the
true teachers from the false? And is not doubt and our own intuition
an essential tool in discrimination?

My first response is that if a teacher says "you are not..." he
distinguishes himself from the disciple, makes him different.
The so-called teacher never emphasizes the not-knowing
because in reality there is nothing to know. To a certain extent
the disciple must trust the teacher and follow his advice, that
is he must make the information his own, first-hand. He
should quickly come to moments of clarity which convince
him that he has found the truth. He must feel himself more
autonomous. If not, he must not stay for secondary reasons,
compensations.

Real doubt is when you know moments of truth, of non-
doubt, and then you fall again in the old patterns. Ask the
question "Who doubts?" and live with it.

Why is it that I have a strong fore-feeling of truth but I cannot be it
constantly?

Be aware of the exact moment when you leave it and you
will discover the mechanism and the circumstances why you
leave it. You are so accustomed to feeling yourself as a center
that this habit contracts you away from your wholeness. You
go away from a vast nothing in order to be a small something.
You go away from your Absence to create a presence.

But if wholeness is complete security and fulfillment and I have
moments of living this, I don't see why it would not instantaneously
break the habit.

To objectify yourself is very deep-rooted. Become aware of the passage between nothing and the desire to be something, between your expansion and being a center. You can feel this passage clearly between the sleeping and waking states. Take note how the body-mind and all its habits wakes up in you, in your emptiness. This is very important.

So before the moment of wholeness the habit is in the dark and afterwards it is still a habit but now seen as one?

Yes, exactly, it is in the light.

Wile meditating must we chase away all the thoughts that come to us? What should we do when they do come? So very often we get caught up in them and let ourselves be carried away.

Ah! So you bring me back to this question which I thought I had already spoken of often. See you live in a dream state. Whether you chase thoughts away or let them carry you away, you end up in exactly the same situation. You remain in the subject/object relation. The doer is reinforced.

Well, what should I do then?

Absolutely nothing. Doing and not doing amount to exactly the same thing. The last thing is to *try* to gain tranquility, to try to become calm.

You have taken note, you have already seen yourself being carried away by your thoughts. Just seeing it implies a transfer of energy away from being lost in your usual thought patterns towards reality. There is already some distance, so as other thoughts occur, quite a different attitude will settle within you and you will eventually find yourself outside the whole process. In the end you will become aware of a current of energy preceding each thought. The continuous swinging between having and becoming will die out too and you will be absorbed into the present, "now." Then there is peace, silence, tranquility, but no personal identity to be silent.

I have taken note for years that thoughts carry me away. If there has been a transfer of energy it has made no difference in my life. I cannot see how simply taking note can be enough, unless of course I am taking note in the wrong way.

Taking note does not mean you jot it down in your mental diary and forget about it. Here you make it a concept. You have emphasized the fact, not the seeing. This is the lazy way, the passive way. Taking note means that you remain alert, you see the fact and the alertness remains after seeing the fact. See how the seeing acts on you, how it feels to be the seer. The background is emphasized. This is where the transfer of energy occurs.

How can we possibly lead an everyday life and "be" at the same time?

Everyday life and 'being" are not two as you still think, because consciousness and its object, action or thought, are one. Everyday life appears in consciousness. You are this consciousness but you are not what appears day after day. Question yourself deeply: To whom do these things appear? Who judges them, condemns them? Who swings between likes and dislikes, and who is it that is also an integral part of what appears? You know the person that refuses, accepts or chooses. You know moments when you make a choice and others free from choice. What you are fundamentally is completely beyond all this.

Distinguish within yourself between the person that is

involved in choosing, who functions from a viewpoint, and the observer who is ever choiceless. Live more and more from the impersonal, and you will one day knowingly be in this impersonal presence. Here, what we call everyday life takes root and flourishes. Here, there is no person bound by fear, desire or anxiety, to intervene or interrupt the natural flow of life. From what you have said you would think that everyday life was nothing but a burden. Who for? Drop the who, and you will soon see that there is no burden to bear.

Can the world exist without desire?

The world exists within you; you are not a part of the world, you give birth to the world. Who desires? The only reason you desire the existence of a world is to reassure yourself, your ego, so that you can believe in its continuity. Where does this desire spring from? It exists for someone who wants to exist and yet finds the world lacking in interest.

So it's not so much desiring the world but searching for something deeper, the desire to be?

Yes, this is the only thing we can hope for, all the rest is compensation.

Is this desire essential?

Yes.

So we mustn't systematically destroy all desire?

No, for it can be a pointer. When we move from one compensation to another, we disperse ourselves. If we see this dispersal for what it is, desire can then be orientated.

Since you have so clearly defined your desire and you have realized that in reality it is a desire *to be*, this implies that you are capable of discriminating. You may have the forefeeling of being without qualification, being without being a father, an actor, a lover, a lawyer, a minister. Being is the origin, prior to all these. Once you feel this deeply, you no longer strive to become this or that, for this would only be another aim, projection or compensation. And what happens when you let go of all becoming? You can no longer refer to anything whatsoever. The past and future are no more... there is only nothingness, silence. This silence cannot be located in space and it is timeless, you are entirely present, and from this perception comes the desire to be.

Why doesn't this silence remain?

It does remain. It always is, but you part company with it.

What I would like is to be able to express what I am.

But you do so constantly, you can never express what you are not.

I get the impression I express nothing but what people have made me.

Well, rid yourself of what others have made of you and you will be what you are. It is possible. Bare yourself completely. Eliminate all acquired characteristics, they are not really you. They are just a lot of habits held in place by memory.

When you garden or drive, you simply function, there is nobody who says "I am digging, I am driving." Where, at that moment, is the person fabricated by others? It is totally absent. It only appears when thought of. It is an idea just like any other. You must see in the moment it happens, the very instant when the "I" pops up and appropriates the action. See it in the moment and change follows effortlessly of its own accord.

Since I saw that much of my life is a compensation for something deeper I have lost interest in my life, even my job and my family. It feels very uncomfortable to stay in the old situation. I feel like Siddhartha, drawn to spend all my time and energy in discovering the real nature of existence. I feel time is short and yet, of course, I cannot simply leave my wife and work even though neither understands my longing. Have you any suggestions?

See that up until now you have put yourself in categories, thought of yourself as a husband, a father, a banker and you have lived going from one state to another. Why identify yourself with all these functions? Why this restriction? When you really see this mechanical behavior a real background will appear in you which will sweep you away from identifying with all these categories. You will be this background in all the functions of life and they will no longer be stuck in a frame, your actions will be free from memory. They may appear completely new to you. You will no longer feel caged or restricted. The different roles in life are in you but you are not in them. They are not you but they belong to you and you are not lost in them.

Only then can there be clear vision and creative behavior.

There may come a moment in life when the world no longer stimulates us and we feel deeply apathetic, even abandoned. This can motivate us towards the search for our real nature beyond appearances. When we no longer find interest in activities and states, when we no longer feel much pleasure in objects and human relationships, we may find ourselves asking: "Is there something wrong with this world or with my attitude towards it?" This serious doubt can lead us to ask: "What is the meaning of existence? What is life? Who am I? What is my true nature?" Sooner or later any intelligent person asks these questions.

As we live with these questions, look at them closely, we become aware that the "me" always seems to be at the center of things playing several roles: "I am cold. I am tired. I am working." With a more open-minded alertness it becomes apparent that the body feels cold, tired, or is working, not "I." In the same way when we look at states: "I wish. I am depressed. I remember. I am bored," we see that we have identified ourselves with the thought or feeling. In looking at this relation between the I and its qualifications it becomes obvious that we have taken it for granted and believe ourselves to be this "me."

This "me" has therefore no continual reality. It is a false appropriation. It lives only in relation to its qualifications, its objects. It is fundamentally unstable. But because we have mistaken our real self for this imposter we feel an insecurity, a doubt, a lack, a sensation of isolation. The "me" can only live in relation to objects so we spend all our energy trying to fulfill the insatiable insecurity of this me. We live in anxiety, fear and desire trying at one and the same time to be as individualistic as possible and to overcome this separateness. The "me" which appears occasionally is taken as a continuum. Actually it is only a crystallization of data and experience held together by memory. Being fractional, its viewpoint is fractional functioning through like and dislike. Its contact with its surroundings is based on this arbitrary choosing. Living in this way is miserable. The loneliness of such an existence may be temporarily camouflaged by compensatory activity but sooner or later, as we said, our real nature will make itself felt and our questioning will become more urgent. We will begin to feel that what we take for the body and mind is not the actual state of things. In deeper inquiry we feel a certain distancing between the inquirer and his environment, activities and opinions. For a time we may feel like an observer of our life, the spectator of the spectacle. Our body and mind are instruments to be used. We observe the changes of the psychosomatic structure as we grow older. We become aware that many, if not most, of our actions are mechanical reactions. All these happenings are seen from the impersonal observer. We begin to feel closer to the knower of these changes and less identified, lost in, the changing. In the end the seeker is found to be what was sought.

What do you mean by that last statement, "the seeker is found to be what was sought?"

You are seeking your real nature. What you are looking for is what you are, not what you will become. What you already are is the answer and the source of the question. In this lies its power of transformation. It is reality, a present actual fact. Looking for something to become is completely conceptual, on the level of ideas. It has no reality and no effective power. The seeker will discover that he is what he seeks and what he seeks is the source of the inquiry.

It seems to me that not everyone who is a seeker has experienced this deep feeling of unfulfillment or abandonment that you talk about.

It's true. There are those who, because of their past, sense the divine anchored deep within them. In these cases there is no motivation. As Meister Eckhart said, "God is seeking himself."

What past do you mean when you say "those who because of their past" sense the divine in them?

It is a poetic formulation which betrays residues of belief in a past incarnation. Of course there is no past incarnation because there is no past. As long as you take yourself for somebody there is incarnation. But some people live with the feeling of what has never been born. They remember the face they had before they were born.

Is knowing our real self what we call transcendental knowledge?

We can never know our real nature, we can only know what we are not. We can never know transcendence, we can only know what we already know. Knowledge of the world of shapes and forms is not true knowledge. Objective knowledge is only superimposed perception, emotion or concept. True knowledge is "being knowledge." It is not objectifiable or perceivable. The desire for this is the motivation, the reason behind all our activities. As we are not conscious of this real motive, our daily activities are generally very dispersed, and we usually need a teacher to guide us, to orientate us towards a better understanding.

The body and mind have no reality in themselves, they are entirely dependent on consciousness. They change constantly. It is the changeless background that allows us to realize this. They appear and disappear within us, within consciousness, but we are not in them. The body and mind come into existence only when we think of them and can thus be seen to be discontinuous.

When we objectify this being knowledge, when we try to frame it in the body and mind, consciousness itself seems to be discontinuous. For the psychologist this is so. But when closely observed we can see clearly and beyond the shadow of a doubt that this is an error. It represents a lack of deep inquiry.

In the waking state or when dreaming we are involved with the object. In deep sleep we are not. But these three states are founded in pure consciousness, the continuum. This continuum is in the interval between two thoughts, two perceptions, or in deep sleep. Generally we emphasize the absence of form. We put the accent on the objective side of the experience, which makes it appear negative. If we did not emphasize the absence of objects we would remember its positive side, the presence of pure consciousness, wholeness.

Any question we might ask ourselves about our true nature springs from the feeling of being, otherwise we could not even imagine the question. It appears spontaneously from the answer itself. Once the seeker loses himself in silence, abandons himself to this fore-feeling of truth, he will discover himself to be this truth. The seeker is what is sought, and what is found. This discovery is not bound by the limits of space and time. It is an immediate insight. In this understanding the adorer loses all dynamism, all volition, and simultaneously his very existence as adorer. He sees himself to be adoration. Once the adorer and adored have disappeared, there is oneness. Then we can speak of true intimacy with ourselves, we know our own truth and essence, our true axis. It is not a case of reducing consciousness to knowledge of a thing but on the contrary instantaneous, direct insight brings consciousness without object. The word transcendence implies its complement, immanence. These are concepts. Living knowledge is not a concept.

What does relationship mean if there is no subject/object, nothing to relate to in relationship?

To you, your surroundings are nothing but an image, an idea or an object. You yourself are an idea, an image or object with which you have identified. Thus your relationship with your surroundings is no more than a relationship between two objects, two ideas, two states. All action on this level is really reaction, recognized as such because it is judged as likeable or dislikeable.

But sometimes you find yourself in the non-state, which is neither of the body nor of the mind. It cannot be located mentally or physically for it is not a thought nor a feeling. When you are free from definition, identification and location there is no separation from your surroundings. In the absence of an I-center all appears in your limitless being. In this non-state there are no surroundings because there is no center of reference to project me and you, peripheries, inner and outer, name and form. For example when you look at a tree or flower, it appears through your senses and you appropriate it by naming it as such and such a species. In the first instance there is perception through the body, in the second instance there is a concept in the mind. But as a percept and concept cannot happen together, when both dissolve, there is only the essence of the tree which you have in common with it. This is love. A scientist therefore stops in the percept or concept but a true poet lets himself be taken beyond these to the tree Itself.

The name and form spring from this eternal background. It is only within this global background that real relationship can exist. From the narrow, fractional standpoint of individuality how can there be true relation? Relation appears in consciousness. From the standpoint of consciousness there is *only* relation with all things. Otherwise there is isolation and separation.

$\mathcal{T}$he spiritual search apparently takes place on different levels but in the end they have a common source, the deep desire to know, to be the knowing. Any talk of a spiritual nature must take this into account and not emphasize the relative differences. The dialogue must point to the ultimate motive at any given moment and it is this motive in the question that is addressed and not the contradiction in the question's formulation.

What can we look for in our first meeting with a teacher that proves to us that our approach is the right one?

The instant truth makes itself felt on the first real contact with a teaching, your whole life takes on another direction. You become aware that you have an entirely new outlook, you feel more independent, your habits, emotions, feelings and decisions become clearer. You feel that your thinking and doing is reorchestrated and freed from all dispersion. This change occurs without the slightest will to do so on the part of the person. This forefeeling of truth is decisive in eliminating what is false. We see clearly how we take ourselves for something that we are not, and how all our actions and thoughts, our ideas of success and failure, real and unreal, come out of this false idea of being. From the new, impersonal point of view only the impersonal real exists. The personality appears as a superimposition on the real. It is a name, a form, limited by time and space, produced by the circumstances.

Truth, that which needs no agent to be known, is inconceivable. It cannot be thought, it can only be lived. The longing to be autonomous, to be conscious without an agent, has its roots in consciousness itself. It is a call from deep within you, from your nearest. It cannot be made an object of desire. Once you understand this, the energy which sustained the unreal will be freed and will return to its source of origin, the ultimate Self, Truth.

Life is nothing but pain and suffering. The world is constantly in mourning. What have you to say to this?

Pain and suffering are felt by an individual. This individual calls the absence of pleasure suffering. But these complementarities are states perceived in consciousness. It is obvious, therefore, that the perceiver is distinct from what is perceived. The person, the individual, the ego, is but an object of perception. It is only by habit and error that we identify ourselves with our perceptions and this is itself the cause of all our suffering.

The person only exists within the pain and pleasure structure. The ego maintains itself by forever seeking the one and running away from the other; it lives in constant choosing, in continual intention. The first insight shows us that all intention, all will is to escape from the suffering incurred by the illusory ego. Choosing, attaining and ambition are a needless projection of energy. The object itself contains neither suffering nor pleasure, but is entirely dependent on the person behind it. Our inability to see all the elements of a situation as simply facts, in other words, to accept the situation, is due to the choices made by the illusory personality. We suffer but suffering and pain are strong pointers, inviting us to inquire just who is suffering.

With the deep desire to ask this question the accent shifts from the perceived to the ultimate perceiver whose nature is joy beyond pleasure or its absence. In this way we could say that suffering leads to joy.

What part is played by thought in the search for truth?

When taken to be a separate entity, thought is used by most people as a tool of aggression and defense. Thought is composed of the past, memory, but is quite capable of realizing its own limitations, and ultimately gives way to its source, stillness, being. It arises from silence and loses itself in silence. Thus its function is to point towards that from which it arises, the ultimate which is unthinkable.

Thoughts are always commandeered by the ego so as to enforce its existence, but isn't the idea of the ego embedded deeper within us than thought?

The ego is nothing but a thought amongst many others. It is a product of memory, of the past. Believing itself to be a separate entity, it protects itself by building a screen and reacts against anything likely to menace this supposed existence, supposed continuity. This belief is the cause of agitation, worry and dispersed activity.

But how can we free ourselves from this phantom and its screen?

The ego struggling to survive either clings onto its accumulated memories, or projects desires into the future, thus using up a considerable amount of energy. Accumulation, choosing, elaborating, all take place on a horizontal plane, in time and duration. The energy constantly turns back upon itself, creating a vicious circle. Being uninvolved with this movement, this dispersal, this sterile swinging between past and future, puts to rest the energies that sustain these habit-patterns, and we finally awake to liberating awareness. Then the energies converge vertically in the eternal now. Only awareness which has nothing to do with mental activity, which is free from all reference to the past, free from bodily and psychological habits, free from selection and repetition can open the door to spontaneous understanding. Instantaneous understanding consumes error and the energy which previously constituted the error shifts away from it and integrates with truth that is being.

Be knowingly silent as often as you can and you will no longer be a prey to the desire to be this or that. You will discover in the everyday events of life the deep meaning behind the fulfilment of the whole, for the ego is totally absent.

Your constant living in strategy, your involved expectations, derive from the anxiety / desire pattern and prevent you from finding what you are searching for, that which in reality has never been lost. Agitated swinging from past to future prevents you from living in fulfilment now. In your natural state, there is no need for reminders because nothing is forgotten.

Thoughts and feelings ebb and flow like the tide, you identify with them and say: "My thoughts, my feelings." The body is a mass of dense sensation more or less localized. The mind is equally a collection of thought-patterns and emotions; but your body and mind are but manifestations of the Self, you exist because you are an expression of pure consciousness. Your nature is to be alert and aware of what appears in you, but you must be knowingly aware, know yourself to be aware. You are the ultimate knower of all things; direct perception awakens you to this living, this being.

You cannot know your true nature through logical analysis.

Letting meditation flower in everyday life brings about its fulfilment.

When we live in the "now" are we always creative?

All potentialities attain fulfilment according to their inner capacity, but we are not these potentialities. Things follow their natural course without any intervention on the part of the person. You are creative when you seek nothing, when you do nothing. Things fulfill themselves within you without your needing to take part intentionally. Give all your heart and intelligence to whatever should present itself from one moment to the next, let every moment die and welcome the next.

I am sure that things fulfill themselves in oneself without any effort when one is already open, but is not a certain amount of concentration needed before one reaches this openness? Otherwise when you say "there is nothing to do" it seems to lead to a passive giving up.

In concentration you anticipate what belongs to the already known. It is the known which veils the surprise. In active acceptance the unexpected comes to you.

When I say, "There's nothing to do," I mean there's nothing to project and no one who does. Live without memory. There is nothing passive in the not-doing. It is supremely alert, a mental and physical readiness, a whole-hearted welcoming of life as it comes to you. This welcoming is not with a view to fatalistic surrender in which there is still the residue of achieving something. It is welcoming for its own sake. Welcoming, openness, is the nature of life.

It seems to me there is thought provoked by memory and spontaneous thought.

Intentional thought makes use of the already known, of memory. Spontaneous thought finds its roots in the ever-pervading source of life.

Sooner or later the thought-patterns elaborated by the ego in its self-defense lose their emotional impact and are reabsorbed into the all-possible of which they are only a part. A mind filled with thoughts concerning the already known is not receptive to the current of life that flows from the all-possible.

Where is memory localized?

Conceptual memory is localized in the brain. It is concretized perception. It is the recognition of name and form. When we live only in concept and recognition we live in abstraction. By abstraction I mean we live separated from the perception, in fraction. The body is not included. The real understanding of things is the total understanding in which the body participates.

There is also organic memory which is maintained in the cells of the body. The body can recall it, but just as conceptual memory abstracts us from the perception of a flower, so we live in abstraction from the perception of our actual body. This organic memory is usually paralyzed by an overactive intellect, an intellect driven by desire and intentional thinking.

What role does meditation play in eliminating the effects of memory?

True meditation means the absence of a meditator and something meditated on, the absence of the subject/object relationship. Only this true meditation, timeless awareness, can free us from the hold exercised by the automatic reactions of thought and memory. This presence frees and regulates —without any desire to do so—the energies engaged in these reactions.

What connection is there between the permanent state and the state of meditation?

The meditative state, our true nature, is not properly speaking a state. It is the very substance, the background to all states. There is no anticipation, no projection, no striving towards a goal or a result. It is silent presence. We can distinguish neither an inside nor an outside, thus we cannot situate it physically or psychologically. Beyond time and space, it is being.

What is meditation? How should we meditate?

First of all, ask yourself why you want to meditate. Don't think about it, just look at whatever should present itself, without trying to extract an answer. You can never meditate intentionally. You can only learn to give up what is not meditation. All effort to eliminate or become is useless because the attempt is itself part of what you are trying to eliminate.

Total understanding, instantaneous awareness, cuts short all intention and the driving force behind it. The stress placed on the object, the uneasiness, fades away without anyone intervening. A silent emptying pervades us. Here there is meditation, fullness and love; in the Ultimate there is no desire either to love or to be loved.

All objects of meditation or adoration, all representations of *Ishtamurti*, are mental creations, projected qualities of the divine which keep us in the subject/object relationship by stimulating our affectivity. Such representations are effective only when the admirer is completely dissolved in the admired so that there remains no emotivity or representation.

Senses and mental faculties, continually coming and going, appearing and disappearing, can never contribute to the experience of the Ultimate, the continuum. The latter transcends thought and senses. Any object is a pointer towards ultimate reality but we must carry it back to its generic form, thus eliminating its changeable nature, to reveal its essence, the living reality with which we are one.

To reach the source, the essence of *Ishtamurti*, form and idea must be entirely abandoned. Many seekers caught up in the subject/object web find themselves confronted by a final object, a blank state. The object has been reduced to its generic form but this undifferentiated potentiality then becomes an object which cannot come home. It always threatens to become again differentiated. There is a certain effort required to maintain this blank state. For those caught in this subtle duality, the blank state becomes a mystery which the mind can never solve. Having reinforced dual conditioning by bringing it to the most subtle levels a seeker can never escape this self-made prison. It is a tragic enigma which only blessed and unexpected circumstances can solve.

Do these blessed circumstances necessarily include the presence of a teacher?

Not necessarily. Life is full of surprises and there are circumstances which may take you out of the mind. For example, in astonishment or admiration you live in the absence of the mind and in your fullness because you are taken outside the subject/object relationship. Such circumstances are rare. A real teacher is also rare but once encountered stimulates the presence which is behind the mind. It is the presence of the teacher which has the power to awaken the non-dual presence of the disciple.

Does the teacher ever act with intention? Does he or she ever use their power to stimulate freedom?

Using any powers belongs to the mind, the ego, and inevitably fixes the disciple in discipleship. This happens very often in the guru world!

It is only in mind relation that there's bondage. In freedom from the mind you live your autonomy. There can be no intention in the sayings or actions of a true teacher.

So the teacher does not free the conflict, he brings the disciple to free himself?

The teacher is established in the non-dual and, through his or her presence and by his sayings, shows the disciple that he is the knower of this enigma. When the disciple is convinced that he is the knower of the blank state, he is open to the new dimension of non-dual presence. In this openness the fixed energy that maintained the blank state dissolves. The words of the teacher come directly from the freedom the disciple most deeply longs for and they awaken this freedom in the disciple. The guru does not free the disciple but brings him to the threshold where freedom abides. The disciple is taken by his own autonomy. Then it seems to him that nothing was attained but that he has always been free. He sees that the blank state belonged to the mind and he is now forever on the other shore.

When you say there is nothing to do or to learn, there is only undoing, unlearning, is it not a game of semantics? It seems that unlearning is a form of learning and a much more difficult learning than acquiring knowledge.

Our natural state needs no learning. There are paths where there is unlearning of wrong learning but this is a progressive way which in the end is still a new learning. Be free from learning and unlearning, doing and not-doing. No volition is necessary to see you are conditioned. In seeing all that you are not in one moment, no other state is projected because it is not possible to conceive of an unconditioned state. So in seeing what is false there is a spontaneous giving up and all that remains is the unconditioned, inconceivable non-state, that you are.

That is why the direct way is so simple, you abide in the seeing and the rest takes care of itself just as eighty percent of our functioning takes charge of itself.

How does discrimination work?

Seeing facts as they are is discrimination but in order to see facts the discriminator must be absent. Discernment thus only takes place when there is no controller, no person to perform it.

What habits reinforce the ego?

Habits such as being attached to things, looking back to the past, recalling past experiences and their emotional content, wishful thinking and daydreaming in search of security for the continuity of the person, all do so. The person is a phe-nomenon of time but being is eternal.

Your true nature transcends the mind and body. This is why the question "Who am I" can never be answered. It has no hold on you: all terms of reference slide away and you awake to all-answering silence. Searching for yourself in any way is a complete waste of time. This must become a perfectly obvious fact to you. Don't endlessly question this self-evidence. Liv-ing is to be found in the timeless "now." So don't accumulate more things, learn new ways to meditate or relax or purify. All this accumulation of states and sensations and techniques is nothing but vanity. It still belongs to the person who looks for security and confirmation. Conflict and problems all derive from the mind as it tries to justify its existence. When you see this suddenly, in the utter conviction of total awareness you become conscious of what you have never ceased to be: the unfathomable bliss of the Self.

In the non-dual state which is not truly speaking a state, there is neither a subject perceiving nor an object perceived; creativity unfolds spontaneously, free from the split mind. States are temporary; they come and go in a background which acts as a support to all the different states that arise. This continuum is ultimate security and peace. If we are lacking in lucidity we are easily led to believe that the peace of this non-state results from action. Therefore we attribute it to something outside ourselves. Spontaneous, clear-sighted vision dissolves all the patterns that produce states and shows us that the non-state is without cause, it exists in itself by itself. Without the object the seeker disappears. All that remains is what was there at the outset. This occurrence can be called enlightenment.

These words can only find their full development and reintegration in non-directed listening. This listening is openness, living meditation. Everything that is heard in this listening points directly towards ultimate reality. This cannot be conceived of in words or thoughts. We feel it in moments during our lives, for example, when in a thought-free state of wonder or astonishment.

The true aim of our existence is to *be*, without conditioning. This is the only way of life promising joy, freedom and peace. There are many ways which lead towards knowing our condition, depending on a person's temperament. However, it is essential that we should not, for one instant, lose sight of the fact that the Self, the continuum, Life, is not a mental or psychic experience and cannot be found on the level of experience or mental exercise. Only a clear mind which knows its limits can free the way for what is beyond it. If the mind remains confused and keeps striving to attain something, however subtle, however open-minded, it will inevitably finish up by turning round and round in circles within the same old structures. Such a so-called progressive approach is totally ineffectual. Deep reflection on ultimate reality is not a question of dialectics but a letting-go of the fractional intellectual hold to make room for an awakening of global consciousness. An experience of this order is beyond all description. It is devoid of all conceptual content. It corresponds to what we are outside of time, and by transcending perception reveals itself as eternity.

Man's essence escapes the qualifications given it by his environment. Once he ceases to identify with the definition given by these surroundings, he discovers himself to be unique and free. Total, living freedom is exempt from all concepts such as the image of the ego. Projecting a "me-image," just like any other object, is conditioned by purely accidental factors but is always dependent on the unchanging ultimate subject: pure consciousness. It is only the imaginary me which feels deprived of liberty. In its absence such a deprivation cannot take root.

Questions concerning the "Who am I?" always derive from a state of disequilibrium. For whom is the world a problem? For whom do pleasure, pain, like and dislike exist? For the me who is but a creation of society, a fictitious entity. When the ego sees this fact quite clearly all its problems vanish. These questions find their answer in enlightenment, the "I am" beyond words, thought and expression. The quest takes you beyond the known, to the back ground of the known. The question here becomes the answer and it is reintegrated into silent awareness.

The ego likes to direct things and circumstances according to its wishes, but its existence is only a shadow dependent on the body-mind that projects it. In the guru's presence, the ego is not rejected, but the clear-sightedness the teacher conveys to us gradually rids us of the characteristics that the ego falsely appropriated. Sooner or later, this clarified ego is reabsorbed into its essence and homeground which is lucid presence. It only appears when called for and never again steals the light for itself.

Enlightenment is instantaneous but the mind becomes gradually clearer. The clarity of the mind brings about a relaxation from old patterns, a freeing of energy which in turn stimulates clearsightedness. It leads us towards living free from all striving to attain something, free from the tension brought about by waiting for something to happen, expectation.

While we listen to the teacher as he sets forth the spiritual perspective, everything seems to be quite clear, free from problems, but afterwards, we seem to leave our true center. Why is this?

As we listen to the teacher talking of the truth, our listening is totally receptive, we are open to what is said. It takes body and life within us. Later, the old patterns of the ego, interrupted as we listened to the guru, take a hold again in everyday life. You must see them to be objects and thus you will spontaneously find yourself outside their field of action. If you do not comply with your old patterns they will be isolated and this will re-install you in your true nature such as you experienced it in the sage's presence. This position, this stepping-stone, will fall away as the experience becomes more and more frequent.

*Can we come closer to understanding reality, "things in themselves",
through word and thought?*

Language and words cannot possibly express what is
inconceivable. Words are at the mercy of an egocentric
empiricism. They find their foundation in the consciousness
from which they arise and to which they return. The ego has
its origins in a mental image: "I am the body."

Spontaneous thought escapes all contradiction, leaves no
samskaras, no residue. Over and above the opposing poles
of beautiful/ugly, good/bad there is a uniting consciousness
which cannot be grasped, nor apprehended by the mind, for it
is beyond all concepts.

We do not know things, we only know them in appearance. To know a thing itself, we must go far beyond its appearance, which is nothing but name and form. We can only see
the reality of a thing when we are that reality: knowledge
without object.

*I know moments where I am completely satisfied, there is nothing
lacking, and I am free from any striving or expectation. Apart from
these rare moments I tend to feel rather gloomy.*

The ego lives in complementarity and is sometimes gloomy
so it seeks pleasure to avoid its opposite "gloominess."
Avoiding gloom is quite impossible, for happiness and gloom
are the heads and tails of the same coin. The moments of
satisfaction you experience are not in a subject/object relationship where you can say "I am free, I am happy." These
moments without thought, dream or representation are our
true nature, fullness, which cannot be projected. It is an
experience encountered where there is neither somebody
experiencing nor a thing experienced. Only this reality is
spiritual. All other states, "highs," whether brought about by

techniques, experiences or drugs, even the so often exalted *samadhi*, are phenomena—and carry with them traces of objectivity. In other words, as what you are is not a state, it is a waste of time and energy chasing more and more experiences in the hope of coming closer to the non-experience.

How can the giving up of experiences happen so that we come to global understanding?

You see that in an experience there is still an experiencer who is stuck in the pattern of going in and out of states. Global understanding is the sudden awareness that the perceiver of these states is unaffected by them, that they appear *in* the perceiver. This insight occurs in a flash when all the fragments preventing us from understanding, yet which point towards it, unfold in the uninvolved witness.

Awareness is the essential element allowing non-understanding to become understanding. It does not result from accumulation as when we learn something, a language or an instrument, for example. It is instantaneous like a flash of lightning where the various elements preceding it are suddenly seen simultaneously and are reorchestrated, just as the particles drawn by a magnet fall into a pattern when they become attached to it. This sudden vision can eliminate all previous problems without leaving the slightest shadow of non-understanding. This resorption into total understanding releases all the energies usually molded into set patterns and opens the way towards ultimate truth, oneness.

Seeing ourselves as an autonomous entity, an individual, is the basic error of our conditioning. This fractional viewpoint makes understanding an impossibility. It is a fictitious concept, totally lacking in substance and independence, just like the images that appear in dreams. Everything we do on the level of the concept "me" is intentional and implicated. Any action influenced by the concept of the individual I, traps us in a vicious circle. In these circumstances we are the doer, the thinker, and are chained in a psychological relationship to the act or thought.

Pure spontaneous action, free from choosing, the action of infinite consciousness, is quite indifferent to conventional morality or immorality, positive or negative. Concepts elaborated from a moralistic point of view only limit the action which in itself is undivided plenitude. When the action occurs spontaneously, it is entirely free of the opposing force that any form of choice implies. Where there is choice there is someone choosing, a viewpoint, doer, thinker. But in truly creative moments, everything takes place without an I interfering. Things occur of their own accord, such action is total action.

When desire arises without having yet found its expression, either in words or as a fixation on an object, we should become conscious of it while remaining completely uninvolved. In this way agitation ceases and the dynamism in it dies away into the observer, the I that contains all and can desire none other than itself. The momentum of the desire is completely felt. It is a striving in the dark towards some form of expression. One must become fully conscious of this desire without its crystallizing in a concept, a direction. This non-directed energy brings us back to our true nature which is objectless. Once we arrive at this clear-sighted vision, nothing appears to be more obvious than the ultimate reality of unlimited consciousness.

Real life is beyond life and death, appearing and disappearing. It cannot be reduced to the mind or limited by memory. Life, concealed in appearance, reveals itself when we clearly see that our habitual living is a compensation. This understanding loses its concreteness and is reabsorbed into stillness. In the realm of the known, everything is qualified, classified and filed away. Beyond the known is never-ending discovery. Everything points towards awareness and is reintegrated in it.

Fear and anxiety are the pawns of memory and the known. Emotional involvement blinds us; it is nothing other than a reaction produced by a psyche cut off from its source. Ideas and ideals are a flight from continual renewal.

When once we take the object as a pointer to what we are, a path opens up before us, it is a starting point towards self-knowledge. From then on life takes on quite a different meaning. The investigation proposed by the teacher leads us intuitively to this self-knowledge. Once oriented we are spontaneously brought towards becoming established in it.

Discursive thought, full of intention, can never lead towards being. Direct intuition of the perspective enlightens us, shows us that there is nothing to be gained by accumulating or acquiring. Then the seeker loses its striving force and dies. As soon as all illusion is dissipated, the seeker is revealed as being the object of his search.

Ultimate harmony depends on establishment in the Self in which the mind, spirit and body are united in harmony. Our whole psychosomatic organism bathes in this well-being and all mental activity is calmed when joy surges forth. At its very first caress let yourself be taken into bliss. Now objects are nothing other than reflections of this joy, this infinite peace, this reality, constantly present, underlying our everyday activities.

Generally what we call "being conscious" in our daily life is a pale reflection of the Self. The essential nature of the Self, Presence, shines forth in the void between two thoughts, two feelings and two states. Generally we ignore the void as an absence of objects, a "loss of consciousness." But eventually we will become conscious of it, even in the presence of objects.

Real questioning is openness to the unknown. It means letting perceptions, objects, express themselves free from all the qualifications that derive from a center, the censoring ego.

If, during these unqualified moments, we remain in contact with tactile or auditory sensation simply as the uninvolved witness, there is no interference or restriction on the sensation and it is reintegrated into the silent onlooker. In this reintegration all traces of object and onlooker subject disappear. What remains is only being, stillness, what we are fundamentally.

What we are, our Self, all-presence, does not exist in time and space. On the plane of existence one can speak of living and dying, which are images created by the mind, but what we are is beyond birth and death. When we talk of birth we mean the birth of the ego, of the me, and by death we mean the death of the ego.

All phenomena evolve in space and time. This is the nature of existence. Existence is in being which is timeless and spaceless. Stopping ourselves wilfully from thinking for a length of time comes from a conceptualized ego and reinforces it. Trying not to conceptualize is also a concept and a violence against existence. Objectifying hinders us, stops us from finding the way to what we really are. All that we can do is become clear that we can never find enlightenment in the realm of thought and concepts. Our true nature is not objectifiable. All striving by the me is a hindrance. When we drop this process all concepts disappear, we are submerged by Grace, and the background, consciousness, becomes a living reality for us.

The Self is silent awareness but this silence is beyond concept and complementarity and cannot be defined in terms of a silence as opposed to noise. Thus trying to rid ourselves of agitation so as to attain a state of silence keeps us in conflict. It keeps us in the realm of opposition, defense, fighting, attaining and rejecting. But if on the contrary we accept the agitation, accept it as an expression of silence, it dissolves in the acceptance. Then you will reach the silence of the Self, beyond silence and agitation. You cannot hope to rid yourself of agitation if you remain on its wavelength, you must listen to it as a whole. It then dies into silence, for it is nothing else but silence.

When we talk of the present, we mean the eternal present, presence to the Self, which is unthinkable, beyond the mind and the psyche.

The seeker can be considered as a projected ego who feels want. Separated from its wholeness it vainly seeks to escape this state of tension. When the futility of the search is seen, it is abandoned and the energy, the driving force, is reabsorbed into the silent observer. The projected energy of the ego which is a centripetal movement, becomes centrifugal. The seeker, who is no longer a prey to the driving force of the search, integrates with what is found, with his true nature which he intuitively knows to be ever present.

Only a conceptualized ego, an objectified I am, can be tied, bound or freed. Once habit and reactions fall away we can no longer speak of freedom or servitude.

All striving to objectify the knower, which cannot be conceived of in terms of concepts, prevents us from directly perceiving our true nature, which is *being*, non-dual knowledge.

All conceptualization, objectification, is a projection of energy, a going away from our nearness where there is neither inside nor outside. It is only the mind that conjures up such ideas as inside and outside, freedom and imprisonment. Such inventions disappear without effort or discipline once they are seen to be imposters. There is being, knowledge and love. It is from this living silence that wafts the perfume of existence.

What place does Grace have in non-duality?

The very moment we obtain a greatly desired object, the ego is extinguished. At this moment both object and ego are absent. It is an absolutely non-dual experience where there is neither observer nor observed. But because we are not aware of it, we bypass it, and only catch a distant echo in our body or mind. We attribute its cause to such-and-such an object. Emotional and physical experiences are no more than states which come and go. Often we confuse non-dual experience with these states. The non-dual experience is beyond subject/object relationship, and strictly speaking is not an experience because it does not need a means to be known. When we see this quite clearly, a forefeeling awakens within us, a reminder that has nothing to do with memory which is a mental function. Following the trail of this forefeeling of our origin, we open ourselves to Grace.

The known object and the knower, the subject, are one. If we consider them to be separate entities this gives rise to the notion of an ego. The doer is an integral part of the object upon which he is acting, just as nervousness and the person who is nervous are one and the same. Once we see this clearly, the wilfulness of the me, the experimenter, fades away into lucid observation, silence, free from choice. Then all potentialities find their expression.

There are many different approaches which question the reality of the world. What should we make of this?

The world is both real and unreal. It seems real when looked at from the point of view of the world, the ego, but when seen from a global view this point of view is restricted and therefore unreal. When consciousness knows itself as the source of the world, the world appears highly real. So just what difference is there between these two realities: that of he who is ignorant of the Self, and that of he who knows himself to be? He who does not know, who takes the perceptible world to be real, limits it to patterns, systems, ideas and beliefs. These all help reassure an insecure ego. But it is a hypothetical world, both restless and passive, a lifeless world. For the one who knows himself to be, the world is an expression of ultimate knowledge. It is a prolongation, an emanation of the totality that is our real nature. The world is constantly recreated from moment to moment, ever new. The world always appears to us according to the point of view we adopt; for the senses it is form, for the mind it is idea, for the Self, the uniting consciousness, it is consciousness.

In this lies the meaning of the Zen saying: First there are mountains, then there are no mountains, then there are mountains again. First the mountains are objects and are called real by the ignorant. Then they are not seen as objects because the subject/object relationship evaporates. But then from the global view they are seen again, not as object mountains but as expressions of oneness. The mountains now appear within totality.

True knowledge is being-knowledge, this is the only knowledge worthy of its name. Truth, being knowledge, is not a part of ordinary thinking which depends on the subject/object relationship. Ordinary thinking stems from the known but being knowledge is outside the realm of having knowledge. It cannot be "had" or "got;" it can only be. If we project the already known, we only close ourselves inside a vicious circle. This attitude will not reveal the unknown, our true nature. Become open to a new dimension. This will immediately result in non-projection, a silence where you are open to reality. Then thinking will lose its boundaries, and its contents will subside into its source, being knowledge.

When an object is recognized as an expression of consciousness, its substance dissolves into knowledge, living silence, peace, lucidity. This light is always there before the object appears. Divided, relative knowledge appears and disappears in undivided consciousness. Thus the appearance of objects is discontinuous but consciousness is constant. Objective knowledge dies away into pure consciousness, global consciousness, and sooner or later you become established in it.

Whatever you do you are always consciousness, it cannot be otherwise. Confusion invades you once you believe yourself to be the doer, the thinker, the willer; but in reality you are purely the witness of your actions.

For example, let us suppose you remember a thought you had yesterday. You are now the witness of this present thought. When you recall a thought about the past it is an entirely new thought, which has nothing whatsoever to do with the thought developed in the past. If you realize that you are the witness of the thought you are remembering, you will cease to confuse the thought with the witness.

How can I free myself from the guile of my thoughts, from repetition? In other words, how can I live creatively?

The mind cannot change itself, the willful ego is only one aspect of the mind. It can never bring about a change by analyzing and choosing, excusing, explaining, criticizing or concluding. Most of the time action is only reaction caused by fear, anxiety and desire. These are aspects of a mind which works like a kaleidoscope which can only rearrange a fixed number of pieces, a mind sustained by the ego, the already known, memory. Through global vision all will, all intention is abandoned leaving only silent awareness, total presence. This silent presence frees us from the patterns fabricated by the ego, thus opening out before us a whole new world of energies.

We divide time into determined periods that we call past, present and future, but when we think of the present it is already part of the past. The only present that really exists is presence. The notion of time comes into existence as thoughts succeed one another. Silent consciousness is ever present, whether we are thinking or not. If things were otherwise, how could we possibly talk of an absence of thought?

Reality becomes a living presence when in non-directed awareness we see error for what it is. It then vanishes, revealing truth and presence. We experience this instantaneously.

It is in this all-present awareness, free of all willing, free of all choosing, that we see error in its true light. Seen in a flash of lightning truth becomes a clear-sighted, luminous certainty. Truth is, and is its own proof, its only proof. It shines forth resplendently, eliminating what is false.

Cause and effect are only a way of thinking common to everyday life. When we think of the cause there is no effect, when we think of the effect, the cause ceases to exist; no two things can exist simultaneously. In the same way, the distinction between subject and object, comparing likes and dislikes, is nothing but memory. Memory is only a thought amongst many others, it has no reality in itself. Whether we think of the past or the future, in reality it is always now. We know time only as a succession of thoughts, based on memory. When we clearly recognize memory as being only a thought, the illusion of time leaves us.

Without an object there is no subject, nor subject without an object. When we are actually perceiving, the subject is absent, it is only afterwards that we say: "I have seen, I have heard." The subject and object are two separate thoughts. We can only entertain one thought, physical activity or sensorial perception at a time. Thought, memory and time arise from still awareness—they are pure expressions of ever present eternity. Each perception is an entirely new world, of which the body and psyche are a part. The world is created anew with every new thought.

We often try to master the mind, to quiet it through concentration, but with clear-sighted vision we soon realize that concentration and distraction belong equally to the divided mind. We cannot possibly master the mind by means of the mind. Concentration only gives rise to a fixation, imprisoned like a canary in a cage. Silent awareness is beyond dispersion and concentration. Once seen in this light, the mind gives up striving and agitation dies away, giving way to living presence.

If we succeed in stopping thoughts by concentration we nonetheless remain in a state of conflict. When the mind is calmed in this way we perceive an emptiness, a feeling of quietness which might mistakenly lead us to believe we had attained the ultimate. It is essential to accept that our true Self is never to be found in a perception, in an object. We can never look in the known for what is beyond the known. If we have a preconceived idea of the ultimate we will try to attain it. This striving itself then becomes the major obstacle. So we must meditate on the sayings of the guru and let their content guide us to non-objective experience. When the object is no longer the center of our attention, attention leaves the object and is reabsorbed into the ultimate subject. This experience is lived quite beyond the ordinary dual relationship of subject and object.

It is the ego itself that creates all our problems for it is at their very root. The teacher helps us to understand this, and then creator and created vanish. As the creator is no more than a projection of the mind, only our true nature remains, ever present, everlasting. We can neither obtain it nor attain it.

All the problems of the world are our own problems, born of the ego. They come and go like waves one after the other. The professionals elected to solve them try to make changes, ignoring who created the problems in the first place. Thus when a change is made in one area the problem erupts in another. In a true approach, we find what fostered the problem, the root of all conflict and we step back. From the impersonal global view the ego together with its problems is reabsorbed into pure consciousness, attentive awareness. Then there are no longer problems and never will be any again. It is only from this global view that intelligence and right action arise, and lasting change can occur.

Are you saying that when we live in consciousness we turn our back on social conflict?

Conflict is entirely due to our fragmented viewpoint. A fragment is always in a state of imbalance. With this as a starting point we can only create more fragments, more conflict and a greater state of imbalance. Sociologists and economists who try to eliminate social conflicts inevitably do no more than create new ones. They consider the conflict to be exterior to the individual when in fact he is the very one to create it. Nothing can be changed from the point of view of society: what we can change is our way of seeing and then we automatically are the most effective member of the society in bringing change.

Once we leave the fragmented view of the ego behind, to take up an impersonal point of view—that of consciousness—conflict subsides. The world in itself cannot be the cause of conflict. We are the ones who build it up out of nothing. Just as long as a man considers himself to be his body, he is a slave to his glands, his bodily functions, his mental projections, to what we could call his conditioning. But if he recognizes the fact that his body has no reality in itself, that is to say, no independence whatsoever, that it is entirely dependent on the perceiver, he comes to realize that the body is no more than an object. In this realization he is no longer an accomplice to the body he inherited. He will see that he is perfect harmony. This corresponds to an impersonal point of view. There is an unfolding, where the body will discover its inner wisdom, consciousness. All activity will now be unprejudiced, unbiased, suited to all situations, conditions and problems.

Consciousness is the hearth from which sparks fly and lose themselves. We erroneously identify with these sparks. They are but fragments. Duality is banished from this hearth.

You said that those who try to change society only reduce one conflict but another inevitably arises. This sounds very abstract. On the practical level surely some changes are better than others? We can't just sit here and say all societies are equally humane or even functional. There must be room for relative change before we are all enlightened. Otherwise self inquiry seems to be a purely selfish way of living. Can you speak about this?

Only a clear vision and deep understanding can bring change. Change comes when you see facts because every situation has its own solution. As long as you look from a personal viewpoint you cannot see facts. So first come to know your own conditioning, the depths of your personal view. Real acting is never personal. When you face a situation impersonally you will be brought to right acting.

You said that from a position free from individual will and choice, we are perfectly able to face whatever situation should present itself. How can this be?

Placing ourselves in a position where we must make a choice creates division. When your starting-point is already divided, it cannot possibly give rise to anything other than further division, which in its turn causes conflict and a state of disequilibrium. A position free from choice implies that you are totally available, receptive to the present moment and open to all possibilities. Any action that follows is born of the harmony implicit in the unity of life, which is free from opposition or contradiction. Nothing exists outside this. It transcends the three divisions of time, past, present and future. It transcends the good/evil duality, situations where we would say I like/dislike, or situations which give rise to negative or positive reactions. We are completely void of memory, in absolute insecurity, but within this insecurity we find everlasting security.

You said earlier that we should meditate on the words of the guru and let their content guide us. What does this mean? And is the content of the words as important as the presence of the guru?

We must let ourselves be completely penetrated by the sayings. As the sayings come from truth the verbal structure dissolves and what remains is the essence which we all have in common. The content of the words is the same as the presence of the guru and our own presence. To be completely penetrated we must not emphasize the words or the guru, the apparent "outside" but listen deeply to how they resonate in us, how they stimulate our own wakefulness. We cannot hold onto the sayings but must let them dissolve so that they can act in us.

Is this acting in us of the words visible or invisible?

Both. The real effective power is invisible because it cannot be perceived but its echo in us can be perceived.

$\mathcal{W}$hen consciousness identifies itself with its object a subject/object relationship is created. Then we can speak of a sufferer and an object of suffering. But the knower of these is not an object.

All perceptions are objects perceived in consciousness. Fear is therefore an object, a perception. Before we name it there is no fear, there is only the direct perception, the sensation. Once we name it we lose touch with the perception and live in the concept, the label, for concepts and perceptions cannot co-exist. The fear is conceptualized by the relative subject which is also an object. This subject has no existence in its own right, it only exists within given circumstances.

Taking oneself to be a person is a habit just like any other. It is the desire to be distinct from one's surroundings, different from others. The person exists when it is formulated as a thought, so we can see that it is nothing but memory. Repetition gives it a hold, a locality in which to situate itself. It is a state of disequilibrium which can only perpetuate itself, creating more fear and anxiety. This repetition gives rise to ready-made situations: we have no money, we are lonely, we are ill... it creates thought-patterns which install themselves in the mind and become cyclic. The person can never rid itself of these.

The ego cut off from its origin is easily filled with fear. We live in fear of suffering; the person is nothing but suffering. This suffering must first be fully felt and it can only be felt when it is accepted. Accepted as a fact, objectively not fatalistically. This scientific acceptance can only take place when there is no psychological relationship with the fear, when it is seen from the impersonal standpoint. When we don't conceptualize fear it leaves us, for we no longer nourish it. It is condemned to die when seen in clear-sighted presence.

The understanding that the ego has no reality in itself springs directly from our true being. It does not result from any effort but is instantaneous, neither discursive nor mental. It brings about total presence, wholeness, where fear has no place.

You said that all perceptions are perceived in consciousness. Does not this mean that consciousness is perceiving, is functioning?

Perceiving is not a function. That is why the perceived leads directly to perceiving. Consciousness is perceiving. You cannot perceive the perceiving because you are it.

What do you mean exactly by "the perceived leads to the perceiving."

It is the shortest way to consciousness. The moment the object gives up its representation we live in silent perceiving where there is nothing seen and nobody seeing. It is non-dual.

How does the object give up its representation?

An artist explores the object. He emphasizes the object. The object is passive and his vision is active, extroverted. The truth-seeker emphasizes the seeing, the welcoming. He does not explore the object as such but uses it only to establish himself in the seeing. The object unfolds in attention, brings you back to attention. The artist is temporarily receptive but this is also goal-oriented. He is looking for something and when he finds it he keeps it. The truth-seeker finds himself only in the looking.

How can we free ourselves from this feeling of anxiety that under-mines us?

Once profoundly convinced that you are neither the doer nor the thinker, you will no longer be restless. Only an object, the insecure ego, can be restless and anxious. You will become aware of a host of energies never dreamed of before. Your relationship with those around you will be perfectly harmonious for you will no longer be seeking a result nor expecting anything in return. You will naturally act for the best, allowing only the circumstances to suggest to you.

All action is brought about by numerous factors and you are only one of them. Once you have understood the part which is yours to play, you will be fully capable of creating a society held together by relationships which do not bind but, on the contrary, free you.

Then what sort of life should we begin leading to reach this ideal society?

First of all you must realize that nobody lives, there is just life. It is the mistaken belief that there is a personality alive which drives you to look for security in objects, to maintain a feeling of continuity, to try and dominate life. The idea of being the doer of your actions is the one and only pitfall preventing you from really living. Life is free, without fear, it follows its natural course. Attune yourself to life, be one with it.

We must come to know our psychosomatic field, become aware of how we function without trying to change. This means facing the facts of our daily life without trying to escape or justify them. We should absolutely take note how all our thoughts and doings come out of a center and involve choice. We must note too the results of the actions of the divided, choosing mind. In this way we come to know ourselves and as society is not separate from us we come to know society. When we become familiar with the impersonal position new aspects appear in the situation which were concealed by opinions, likes and dislikes. These additions completely change the chess board.

For me sadhana is this coming to know your functioning, facing the facts of life.

I think I understand what you are saying, but I don't see how I can avoid the conflicts that continuously harass me.

Conflict arises when you think you are this or that. This mistaken identification restricts you. You want to solve a problem by finding an answer in the past, in memory, in what you know. But the past is composed of experiences based on pleasure, pain, hope and all the other illusions of the ego. Free yourself from this pattern of desire and fear. All your problems derive from it. The solution to present problems does not lie in referring to your past, but in seeing the facts of the situation from the widest possible view.

The ego is nothing but memory, a set of definitions which are limiting. You strongly believe in these patterns you have yourself brought about and you mechanically repeat them. It is only habit that maintains them, makes them seem permanent. Let them go now forever.

Does all conflict disappear when one lives without the ego?

A conflict is for somebody. Who is left to remain in conflict?

You know that awareness without tension, where you are uninvolved and do not seek a conclusion, is total awareness. It is this awareness that enables you to see things clearly within yourself. All intention to manipulate the future comes from a partial point of view, that of the ego. Inevitably it breeds conflict. In total awareness the ego and its conflict disappear. When you try to solve a problem by referring to the past, the already known, memory, you may feel appeased for a while but this contentment is based on fabrication and cannot last. You continue to live in the shadow, the threat of conflict. There can be no lasting peace through trying to compromise the ego.

I cannot live in this meditative state, I am constantly distracted by other preoccupations. How can I avoid being distracted from the essential?

The meditative state is a state of being. It means we are choicelessly aware of the life within us, of our surroundings. It is not a divided state where striving is necessary. Culture, education, social and economic factors have conditioned our body and mind, creating fixed mental patterns. All this is at work within us, but we are not identified with it. Our true being is neither implicated in nor influenced by these limits. It is completely free. Once we realize this, an entirely new dimension opens up before us, duality comes to an end, the doer and what is done completely vanish, the object/subject relationship dies leaving no residue.

When does the question "Who am I?" make itself felt most strongly?

Although the question "Who am I?" may be stimulated by a crisis in life, it does not result from a setback, the loss of material possessions or an intellectual disappointment, it springs directly from the inner self. It is beyond time, free from cause, free from striving —for all motivation is inhibitive.

The inquiring state frees all the latent energies within us. The flow of these energies was obstructed on all levels by the rigidity of the ego. Their release is born in us with the presentiment of reality. The question "Who am I?" is entirely free of emotional excitement, which would only hinder the freeing and integration in choiceless awareness of these energies.

The desire to be, to be the living answer, stems directly from the Self, the answer itself. Thus the question "Who am I?" cannot arise in the mind. It has nothing to do with memory. All memory is absorbed by the living inquiry which takes place only in the present moment. Awakening is neither immediate nor gradual, it is instantaneous apperception. The One—which we are—is beyond time. When the mind realizes this, it loses its fear and desire—desire which oscillates between having and becoming.

Living is then that shining lucidity which reveals itself as autonomous, everlasting fulfillment. It is the all-presence in which the waking, dreaming and deep sleep states appear and disappear.

What kind of memory is meant by the saying, "Remember the face you had before you were born"?

When you try to remember the face before you were born you cannot. This frees you from all representation, from memory. In this absence of any representation you glimpse yourself, your is-ness or suchness which is an objectless dimension. In the extinction of being something, of your temporal birth, you find that what you are is never born and never dies.

So in "remembering" the unborn we use memory to come to the extinction of memory.

But it is often said, as Wordsworth phrased it, "Our birth is a for-getting..." and our re-birth is a remembering.

The glimpse of what we are is not a remembering, it is a recognition.

Could you speak of deep sleep? How can we be aware in this state?

Awareness is not in a state. States are in awareness. It is only awareness which makes states possible. Deep sleep is the purest expression of the Self because it is not in duality. What we call deep sleep does not last very long—if we can talk in terms of time—and in the semi-sleep in which we subsequently find ourselves we return to the subject/object relationship.

Because we do not know ourselves except in relation to objects we always strive to find ourselves in relation to objects. We constantly want to choose, control, arrange, classify, qualify. This is a tremendous waste of energy. In clear awareness you know that there is no sleeper, no entity rejoicing or suffering. You *are* that clear awareness in which objects lose their impact. With the deep understanding that the doer, the willer, is an illusion, you will find yourself in complete stillness following an act or a thought. Your sleep will take on a new peacefulness and then the idea of recuperating whilst sleeping will change.

First of all you will no longer dream, because dreaming is only an extension of the waking state, of the frustrations and defenses that have not been thoroughly lived in waking life. This of course will not prevent you from having certain dreams where you are no longer involved, where you are purely a spectator. Without any intervention on your part you will find yourself sleeping much more deeply and just the right length of time for you to be fully rested.

In the evening when you go to bed prepare yourself, so as to avoid taking your daily worries with you. Observe whatever presents itself without becoming involved in the observation. For example, if you feel tired, really look at it and you will spontaneously find yourself uninvolved in it. Sooner or later the tiredness will cease to be the focal point of your attention and will disappear, burnt up by this awareness. Do the same with all the worries that preoccupy you. You will come to experience a feeling of harmony. Finally let your body sink into deep sleep.

When you wake up in the morning, don't go immediately into a relation with objects. Stay in that moment before the old patterns return. It is your true being. First of all be deeply aware, let the ego and the world come to life later *in* your awareness.

When your body feels exhausted it is generally a result of your continual reacting. Once you are free of the ego, you will no longer feel tired, you will be free of all set patterns for they will not be able to take a hold on you. Of their own accord they will find their own conclusion within you. You will become much more supple when confronted by things which used to bother you, you will no longer feel overburdened by them but will recognize them to be purely mental patterns, cliches providing a false sense of security and stopping you from feeling fully alive.

Isn't it advisable to sleep less? Isn't this constant want of rest only a compensation?

If you wilfully try to sleep less, you are only imposing a discipline upon yourself. This is ridiculous, and of no interest at all from our standpoint. Sleep normally according to your body's needs, it knows its needs better than you do.

You mentioned uninvolved dreaming. What distinction do you make between uninvolved dreaming and dreaming?

Dreams, as I said earlier, are a means of eliminating reactions which were not fully lived in the waking state. The dreaming and waking states are identical in that you don't know yourself in either but know yourself only in objects. While you are dreaming the objects are real for you. Only when in the waking state do you say "I have dreamed" but your relation with the dream apple or waking apple is exactly the same subject/object relation.

In the uninvolved dream, the spontaneous dream that is not composed solely of the day's residues, the subject-ego is absent and these dreams are the only important dreams, doorways to your global being.

Sometimes in the moment between being asleep and being awake before you have gone back into the old patterns there may be an instantaneous feeling of being in reality, enabling you to understand this reality beyond analysis. To live this reality in the waking state is like an uninvolved dream where there are no objects or subjects.

I do not understand what you said about waking up, not to an object but to what we are intrinsically. Waking up, to me, is just that: the return of the objects.

I was not speaking of waking up to the everyday world of objects but of the awakening in our real nature. This is the only thing we are concerned with here.

It gradually dawns upon us that we are not the person, that we are this awareness; this becomes more and more tangible. When we really wake up what we previously called being awake seems also like a dream.

Can this non-dual experience be felt in the waking state, in daily life?

Yes. It can come about quite unpredictably. Suddenly we feel a letting-go. We are no longer impelled to action by outside circumstances. Abruptly we become aware and the mind is calm, it returns to stillness. Don't let these moments go by or take them for simply an absence of objects. You will be often invited by them, for example, before the appearing of a thought or action and after its disappearing. You may even be solicited during action, when you feel the action is in you but you are not in the action. Be alert for these invitations.

Can we describe awareness?

No, we can express it in living but we cannot put it into words. All action which arises spontaneously subsequently takes place in time and space, calling upon your intelligence to carry it through to its accomplishment. Only in the complete absence of yourself is there total presence.

There are quite a few who are very lucid intellectually, who have, as you have said, a clear geometrical representation of truth. They may, after living like this for some time, believe themselves to be enlightened. The majority of teachers I have met are stuck here. What can you say about this? How can a seeker recognize one who is clear intellectually from one who knows his real nature? Can the intellectual guide be helpful? And how can one avoid or come out of this trap?

Yes, they have conceptualized the understanding and it has not become being understanding. The only way out is to be aware of what has happened, to face it in humility and simplicity free from the ego.

The seeker can observe whether the teacher has transposed his intellectual clarity into daily living. But the real test is whether the seeker finds himself becoming more independent or more bound to the so-called teacher.

In India there is a group of guides called upagurus who prepare the disciple for the ultimate guru.

You have said, "Live as if you were consciousness, as if you were enlightened. "Is there not a great danger in this advice?

When I said this it belonged to that moment. It was used to effect understanding into transposition in living, or to dissolve the "I am not free" idea. I don't exactly remember because it was a pedagogical saying that appeared at the moment. Of course ultimately both freedom and non-freedom are concepts. But to say "act as if you are free" is very striking. It stimulates spontaneous acting, function without a doer.

Stillness does not mean a peaceful mind, for a peaceful mind is something and stillness is no-thing. The mind can be temporarily calm but this is not stillness. Once we have awakened to the stillness beyond the mind, the latter will cease to be agitated, it will be reduced to its function, that is to movement. Stillness is not in the slightest way affected by this movement. It is inaccurate to say that in stillness there is no longer mind-function. It is the nature of the mind to move although there may be spontaneous moments of non-movement when the mind is suspended in wonder, astonishment or admiration or any unexpected appearance that finds no reference to previous experience, or the moment after a desired object is obtained. Function and non-function belong to the mind but they appear and disappear in stillness which is not a function.

Agitation is produced by desire, the desire of the individual me to bring an end to its isolation, its separation from its origin. In its distress it tries every imaginable means to create pleasure and security. It ultimately longs for joy. Though moments of pleasure and satisfaction are reflections of ultimate fulfillment they remain conditioned by time and space. They are temporary and there is always the fear that loneliness and emptiness will return.

Once the ego sees that it only seeks what it already knows, that its desires are conditioned and that its true desire is for permanent security and tranquility, it loses its dynamism to find itself in phenomenal things. Then what is behind the desire, the ego, the mind, is revealed. We are left in wonder and all dispersed activity dissolves in this wonderment.

How can I get rid of troublesome ideas?

Such ideas, accumulations from the past, appear without being asked. If we intervene or control them, this only pro-longs them. The person wishing to control is of the same nature as the object he wants to control. If we do not inter-vene the emphasis leaves them and they are reabsorbed into our silent observation.

Is the upward path (which strives step by step towards realization) in any way compatible with the approach you are talking about?

Listening does not depend on the level, whatever that level might be. Trying to exalt one level, or pass from one to another, is utterly useless.

How can we come to realize that we only seek what we already know?

When we seek we have a goal, we are seeking a result. This goal is based on the already known. It thus prevents us from being completely open to the unknown, to the completely new.

All thought is memory and is always expressed in terms of the senses. Thought is dependent upon the time and space framework, it appears and disappears and can thus be seen to be discontinuous. But this framework in turn depends entirely on the timeless, spaceless continuum, our true nature, which is eternal, ever there beyond birth and death.

The Ideals of Beauty, Truth and the Good spring directly from our home-ground. The representation arises from silence itself not from any known representation. Like creative thinking these archetypes do not begin with the phenomenal known but with being knowing. They do not arise from the mind but from the conviction of being.

So if we live with these Ideals without representing them or reducing them to common, fashionable notions of good, truth and beauty, they can lead us towards absolute freedom?

These original feelings do not need to be codified because they belong to our fundamental structure of Thinking, Feeling and Willing. In living with them they are spontaneously expressed in daily life. They have nothing to do with the becoming process, becoming beautiful or good but express themselves from moment to moment.

Hindu tradition tells us that all our suffering originates in avidya. What is avidya?

Avidya is the identification with what we are not, our physical and mental functions. Through clear-sighted vision we realize that these functions are inevitably dependent on their knower: vidya. When the accent is displaced from the object with which we have identified, the ego—the state, thought or function—we find ourselves spontaneously in silent listening, in non-function, in being the knowing. What we deeply are becomes living presence. What was previously seen as ignorance is now experienced as an expression of knowing. Everything is an expression of silence. There is no more complementary thinking. Being the knowledge wipes out the duality of knowledge and ignorance.

Could you talk to us about the suffering that results from fragmentation?

Events can be interpreted on many different levels, can be elaborated in many different ways, but this manipulation can never be a way out of suffering. It is the object, the body-mind which suffers, but what we are is the *knower* of the suffering. The moment we recognize ourselves as the knower and not "the suffering one" all psychological pain disappears. Physical pain, when seen objectively, is dramatically reduced.

Believing oneself to be somebody, an independent person, objectifying, projecting, are all objects amongst others, they are pure imagination. Projection is but a fraction of the whole. Taking decisions and thinking from this divided, fractional point of view, can only give rise to a fragmented result. A fraction is a state of imbalance and imbalance can neither achieve nor create a state of equilibrium. We cannot possibly understand the greater by the lesser. Fractions cause insecurity, suffering and a lack of plenitude. However, this feeling of lack originates in the forefeeling of plenitude and is intuitively conscious of it. Desire or lack lead back to their source. If there were no reminder, nor intuition of its origin, there could be no desire. This is where we need a master to point out to us that all objects point the way back to our true being.

Could you talk about listening and its origin?

To discover your innermost being you must start from where you are at this very moment, *wherever* that is. You cannot begin anywhere else. Whatever appears before you—your body, sensations, feelings , thoughts, etc.—must be accepted, listened to as a whole. This does not mean you should analyze, interpret, understand or look for an inner meaning. What is important is to discover listening itself, which sooner or later will be revealed to you. At first the accent is on what is listened to, the sensation, feeling or thought. But the more the listening is sustained the more the emphasis is shifted to this listening itself without a listened to. Then you are at the threshold of the source from which the listening derives. That very instant listening will become a living reality.

Real listening can be neither improved nor perfected, for it is perfection itself. It reveals itself when the mind is struck by wonder, when it no longer refers to the slightest object. This fulfillment is later erroneously attributed to an object but one who is aware of the true perspective knows that the cause of this peacefulness is not to be found in an object, but is a pure reflection of silence, of what Is.

Listening arises from wonderment, to which it also points—a state where there is no projection, where nothing appears. It is as if you had suddenly opened the windows of a dark room full of objects, and in streams daylight. Everything becomes clear in an instant.

What difference does it make whether we intellectually understand the teaching or not? I prefer to just sit in your presence.

When you emphasize intellectual understanding you can never understand. Your understanding is dead. You must go further: When the intellect has really understood it knows that it has no more role to play and spontaneously eliminates itself. Then you live in open light.

The presence of the teacher is the mirror of your own presence, reminds you of it. When you sit and fix the stillness, make a perception of it, you may become relaxed, but you can never come to real stillness. Localizing yourself in a state or focusing on the presence of the teacher you are not open to direct transmission. Only to know that all that can be perceived has no reality in itself. When this has been clearly seen, it is the perspective which opens the unknown region of what we are. There are marvelous moments such as we spoke of before, moments when the mind is suspended. For someone who is aware of the perspective, the thought-free state is not felt as the absence of something but as his own presence. Here the light behind the mind shines forth. Otherwise these moments are experienced as blanks or absent-mindedness, absence of function. The one who knows presence, joy without object, is free from all expectation, all dynamism to "fill the emptiness" and welcomes the experience of pure being. Expectation, anticipation, destroy openness. Imagine you have lived for many years with a Persian rug and one day you send it away to be cleaned. It may take time before you can really see the floor because you see only the absence of the carpet. So come to the absence of the absence.

It is only through living self-knowledge that our energy and possibilities are harmoniously orchestrated. Otherwise there is dispersion and living in the becoming process, end-gaining and ambition. An ambitious mind can never be a free mind.

All intentions aim at finding pleasure and security and escaping from a projected suffering. Many books have been written and many techniques proposed on how to escape from dis-ease, discomfort, but these proposals take for a fact what is fiction. To come out of the endless round of the pleasure-pain structure we must learn to face the fact, the perception, and not deal with the concept.

Listening implies recognizing that pleasure and pain are both part of the same process experienced on the same level. They have their relative existence in timeless joy. Plenitude is the background to pleasure, pain, sadness and satisfaction.

These are all mind stuffs. If we examine them with uninvolved attention the complements converge and dissolve in their source, which is joy without object.

$\mathcal{W}$hatever we do or think, we *are* awareness, so why try to be or think it? If we were not aware we could not take note of the states we find ourselves in. If awareness were only a mental function like all others it would disappear like all functions. But it never disappears. I cannot prove this to you without argument. Being it is proof. But I can tell you how to discover it. So trust me! It will be second-hand information at first but don't remain in belief. Make it your own.

This awareness is present in deep sleep and in the interval between two thoughts. The pure consciousness we name "I am" is beyond mind and body. It is not subject to discontinuity. All sensation and facts are entirely dependent upon this pure reality. We can imagine absence of feeling, absence of perception but never absence of consciousness. You will find this difficult to understand as long as you have not experienced eternal presence.

The world consists of shapes and names. It is brought into being by your thoughts and senses. The world is only there because you are there, the eternal present, the unchanging "I am."

Perceiving is entirely independent of the perceiver and of the perceived object, which are but concepts. Perception is living, the only reality, now. Each perception is a non-dual experiencing of pure awareness. Subsequently we may say: "I

thought this or that," or "I heard a chord in C major" but at
the actual time, there was no thought, only the perception
appearing in the "I am." With deep conviction, this fact will
take root within us and we will no longer need to make an
effort to remember it. It is this true understanding that turns
the "I am" into a reality.

Can you say more about how to live the "I am"?

The "I am" shines in its glory when you are free from the two
volitions: doing and not doing.

What signs are there to guide us towards self knowing?

Since the sensory organs cannot function without the brain,
objects known to our senses are likewise dependent on it.
Seen from this angle the world is a projection of the mind. The
mind exists within awareness. Its very nature is to express
this awareness by means of name and form. Everything that
appears to the mind appears in global awareness. It is this
insight that shifts the accent from the object towards awareness, often called the ultimate subject "I am."

How can we cease believing in total disappearance after death?

You will find the answer by inquiring first: What is life? You
can become aware of the appearance of the body but you can
never become aware of the appearance of life because you
are life. So inquire about life and you will discover that the
inquiring is life itself. We take so many risks with our body.
Think of the sailor or the voluntary warrior. Would he take
such risks if he truly believed in death? He knows without
knowing it that it is only the body which dies, that his vital
self is beyond life and death.

What is this self? Who am I?

Your real nature is stillness, light, expansion without center or periphery. It is unconditioned being, love. But you do not see it for you are a prisoner of your imagination and of second-hand information. You have enclosed yourself in a universe of concepts and beliefs. The ego is only a function, and to identify with it is a lack of true vision. Thoughts, feelings and actions appear in succession before the witness, leaving their imprint in your brain. Recalling them makes you believe in a continuity which is actually non-existent. But memory is a present thought, thoughts of the past occur in the present. In reality there is only presence, non-dual consciousness. We mistakenly take ourselves to be this or that, but there is only the true "I am" beyond time and space.

What is the real nature of the mistake I have made?

Desiring something which is nothing but an illusion, which has no foundation whatsoever; being afraid of truth, which is pure awareness free of thought.

Why would I be afraid of truth?

Because truth is life and you are afraid of living. You take yourself for an object which is born and dies, and you fear dying because you do not know life. It is only an object which is afraid and this object tries by all means to free itself. See that the effort to become free belongs to the belief in an object. The moment you see it turn your head and look behind.

On what level can we find the true answer?

Any question about ultimate reality that seeks an answer on

the phenomenal plane is a pure waste of energy. The right question is the answer. The right question does not come from the intellect, books or hearsay. How, why, when, are all questions which stem from the ego. The latter is purely a figment of the imagination, and it constantly seeks an explanation on its own level. There is no answer to be found on this level. A true question is one that arises in the moment itself. It is resplendently new and contains a foretaste of the answer. The reply comes unexpectedly from the living Answer. It is stillness; it cannot be thought. To receive it we must be open to it, listening without referring to past experience. This openness is the key, it is the nature of the question and the answer. Openness is our real nature.

How can I stand back and observe myself and the different situations that appear? In other words, how can I be a spectator and not feel involved?

You are not the doer, the thinker that rejoices and suffers. Take this for a fact and do not try to be a spectator, to be detached. The fact that you can recall your previous acts proves that you were a witness to them. So above all do not *try* to be a witness—this would only be projection, and would keep you in the frame of ideas and expectations. If you accept this a change will come about within you, probably without your even realizing it at the time it occurs.

The witness is only a crutch to bring you to understand that you are not a doer. Once you are free from doership there will be a change of axis and the energy once directed towards the object will shift to the subject aspect, to the witnessing. In the end all residues of subjectivity dissolve and the witness with them. You discover yourself as that in which the object and subject exist, but you are neither one nor the other. Then there is only living silence.

Are you trying to make us realize that it is identification with the body that binds us to objects, to situations and to the world?

Your true nature is obscured because you believe yourself to be independent, a separate entity. This is what binds you and keeps you living in the pleasure-pain cycle. See that renouncing and aspiring are two faces of the same coin. As long as you believe you are the body-mind you will see forms and shapes around you which are no more than images in juxtaposition with each other. What reality could such a process possibly have? As pure consciousness, you are out of the subject/object cycle and you enjoy the real relationship that only comes in living non-relation.

But discomfort often brings us back to our bodies.

Who knows the body when it is tired or rested?

I do.

Who is this I? Nothing other than the mind. And who knows the mind? The true "I." The mind is simply an activity which comes and goes. The witness records this lack of continuity: body and mind are only perceptions and concepts. Silent non-directed attention reveals this to you and as a result you are filled with living presence: you live in awareness, which is sacred. This is your true nature.

How can I be sure it is not just another state that my ego has created?

In this non-state there is neither desire nor anxiety.

*P*roblems cannot be solved through choosing and deciding. Opinions arise from the fractional mind. When the I is absent the situation presents itself to you as a collection of facts. When there is no one involved in these facts right action appears spontaneously. Seeing all the facts calls for acceptance. Where there is no longer psychological involvement there are no opposing factors and therefore no choices of some facts, some elements over others. Acceptance does not come from the body-mind, it comes from our wholeness. Once all the elements of the situation are welcomed in our acceptance free from qualifying, the situation itself calls for action, but we do not go to it already armed.

The society we live in is full of suffering. I find it difficult to resign myself to this fact.

From your viewpoint, you cannot possibly accept this. As I have often said, you cannot experience pleasure without also experiencing suffering; you cannot have one without the other. You feel sorry for the sufferings of society but don't realize that you are the cause of the suffering. So begin by feeling sorry for yourself!

How can we possible accept ourselves entirely?

Refusal to accept implies defense and aggression: you isolate yourself, cut yourself off from your environment-it is as if you had cut the vital thread of life. Acceptance is our inherent state, non-acceptance is artificial, fabricated. We do not need to force ourselves to accept, simply recognize this fact. If you see this non-acceptance clearly at different moments of the day, you will be outside the process. The energies thus fixated in non-acceptance or dispersed in various methods of escape will return to their source. Once you live in your natural state of observing, your acts will no longer leave any trace within you. You will know when the situation has been totally accepted, fully experienced because you feel entirely free from it. It appears within your freedom.

Where does this fear that so often invades me come from?

Fear comes from memory. It is an object. It only appears in relation to certain situations, certain experiences. It has no more a reality than the ego. You cannot think in terms of "I" without thinking of the situation to which it refers. It is inherent that the human condition try to locate itself somewhere, in a bodily sensation or a thought. But there are moments in life when we ask: do I have any existence beyond this relation to objects or can I possibly know myself in any other way? If we let things flow freely, we will discover ourselves *to be* observation. Knowing oneself is not limited by a subject/object relationship, by an observer/observed pattern, it is a state of joy, of peace, bliss, constant security.

You said that true understanding brings an attitude of total accep-tance. I am 35 and am dying of Aids. How can I face up to this seemingly unacceptable fact?

When you say it is not acceptable see in one moment what

you mean by "not acceptable."

Not just unacceptable for me but also for my family.

See the illness objectively, as if in front of you so that you are not lost in it. Look at your body as if it belonged to another. Then you will have a glimpse of freedom from the burden of it, a moment of psychological space. Become interested in this feeling of freedom, and it will be effortlessly sustained. It is only from this free perspective that you can act most correctly. You are not the body, neither the healthy nor the unhealthy body. So your illness is a gift to come more quickly to realize what you are not. This attitude, which is not an attitude because it comes from wholeness, from Life, will stimulate your surroundings, your family and friends. It will stimulate the Life in them. Knowingly or unknowingly they will share Life with you and neither you nor they will feel isolated. This feeling of Life will remain after the disappearance of what you are not, the physical body. Life is eternal and in it all are in oneness.

There is no illness. Illness is nothing but an accident. In reality there is only health. The very word, the idea of illness already predisposes you to being ill, creates it even. As soon as we classify our sensations into categories so as to name them, our imagination, charged with emotivity, already very vivid in this field, feeds what we could call a malfunction.

You should never name this malfunction, for this only feeds the imagination and confirms your illness. This in itself prolongs the malfunction. In my view, malfunction is a signpost.

The best way to bring a malfunction to an end on either the physical or psychological plane is not to refuse the sensation, the perception. You must accept it but this does not mean accepting it morally or psychologically both of which are a kind of fatalism. Accept it totally, actively. Acceptance is lucid, watchful awareness in which all the facts are seen. It is this acceptance of the facts of the situation that brings about the cure. When you live in accepting, illness no longer has any substance, and you have then the greatest possible chance of getting better. Non-acceptance prevents all possibility of a cure being brought about.

So, the first thing a doctor must do is instill in the patient the correct attitude so that he can live with himself. Clear seeing of all the elements of the situation comes when there is no involvement in the perception, when it is seen objectively. This uninvolvement is the first step towards freeing ourselves. It is only when all the facts have been seen that creative action occurs.

You said that acceptance brings about the cure but you also give suggestions for things to do to help healing. Would you say that only when we accept can we really know what needs to be done?

In acceptance intelligence and right action appear. Acceptance liberates all potential.

Is illness often psychological?

Yes, often. I would say as long as we continue to believe the person exists, we will encounter psychological problems which produce physical reactions. The person shuts itself in a stronghold of aggression and self-defense. This structure is nothing but fear, desire and anxiety. It is an intricate barrier to the natural flow of life within us. This natural flow of life can take care of itself perfectly well, it does not need the person.

Illness, malfunction, result from this opposition.

Does the body heal itself?

A cell became a cell through health. If the cell had no memory of this state of health, it could not cure itself. It knows itself when healthy and there is no need to intervene.

One must help the cell to recuperate. The first step is acceptance of the actual state of the cell, the body. Acceptance means objectifying the sensation, not trying to escape it, dominate it or suppress it. In this total acceptance the body regains its health for it already knows health.

How can I go beyond the depressed states I sometimes feel?

Let us take a few examples. Imagine sitting quietly without any particular aim, secure and with a contented feeling, free from any particular desire to be or do anything. You neither look back over things, nor criticize; you contemplate yourself and find yourself likeable, you are completely absorbed in presence even when there is a bodily absence.

Let us take another example. Through one-pointed concentration, we create a void, an impression of emptiness, but this is still an observer/observed relationship. Someone who is not directly oriented towards the ultimate non-relationship would remain in this state, which in the end only results in a hollow feeling of lack. When, on the contrary, we know that we can never find what we are seeking in an object, no matter how subtle, then our attention shifts from the state to the observation itself, the absolute, global emptiness within which blissful plenitude now awakens.

Does the object exist before we think of it?

That is a purely hypothetical question, an intellectual question. The object appears in you and disappears in you. It is because you are. It is created the moment you think of it.

How does the Self awaken within us?

It is always awake, it is we who are asleep. We are awake in objects but not in the Self.

Reality hides behind its own creation, behind the energy it sends forth. It reveals itself by its own grace; it cannot possibly be attained by action, man appears within this absolute, this awareness that we experience spontaneously without there being a reason. There is only resplendent oneness.

What difference do you see between awareness that is not oriented towards the absolute and which only faces objects and the awareness that points directly to the ultimate subject?

Someone who is not oriented easily loses himself in all sorts of distractions and activities which result from the desire to accumulate, to own things, in the belief that existence consists in doing things, in becoming. The orientated person ignores his ego and when it is no longer paid attention, it dies.

When you are attentive to something you are fixed on the object but when you are simply in attention you are free from all grasping. There is a deep relaxation which comes from the ultimate itself and in which all your being unfolds effortlessly and joyfully. Here the Self refers to itself.

If I have understood you correctly, there exist consciousness of objects, what Atmananda Krishna Menon called functional consciousness, and pure consciousness. I don't understand how there can be two types of consciousness in oneness.

In modern psychology, consciousness is always focused on an object. We claim we are conscious of a thing, so that the interval between two perceptions is considered to be a nothingness and deep sleep is also considered to be a nothingness.

Here, on the contrary, when we talk of consciousness, we know that between two perceptions we are totally present to our true nature; likewise deep sleep is free from all intentional activity and we are being, pure consciousness beyond time and space. Don't try to understand this intellectually; thinking about it is absolutely useless for there is nothing to be found. You can only live this pure presence, which is always. Pure consciousness expresses itself in functional consciousness which can be said to be already in view to perceive. Openness to itself is pure consciousness, openness to objects is functional consciousness. But these are not two, they are the same.

So if pure consciousness is without objects is this not an abstraction?

It is an abstraction as long as you do not live it. The timeless presence, the background behind and between perceptions, thoughts, is pure consciousness. Thinking, perceiving is functional consciousness. Pure consciousness is continuous, its functioning is discontinuous.

It would seem then that one needs a body and a mind for functional consciousness, that it is born and dies, but pure consciousness is before we are born and never dies?

Yes.

So functional consciousness is the tool by which pure consciousness becomes known?

It is through the known that the unknown reveals itself. But there are not two. The ultimate expresses itself in space and time and dies back in itself. The divine enjoys its own expression. It is the divine play without purpose.

Yes, when I see a child playing I never question it. Why analyze the divine play?

It's only the mind that asks questions!

$\mathcal{W}$hat we call the Self is not a soul-like thing, a state, it is the uninterrupted flow of life. We cannot apprehend it with the faculties we use every day such as impressions, feelings or memory, which belong to the fractional, objective point of view. We cannot think it because we are it. In the silence that is beatitude, directed energies such as concepts of time, space and the individual memory leave no trace. Things are lost in consciousness but consciousness is not lost in them. Thus activities go on and we remain firmly established in our true being.

This living joy accompanies each of its expressions. As I said earlier functional consciousness is a prolongation of and one with pure consciousness. The average human being is only capable of perceiving the coarsely apparent side of things, for he is completely dominated by the relative subjective aspect of his experience. Joy obtained by this means is but a fragile interval between two moments of suffering. A headache or a disappointment easily cause it to disappear. True joy is not linked to outside circumstances, it flows directly from the Self. You will be convinced of this if you become aware of these moments of calm experienced before fear and desire take hold.

In what way can yoga help us?

We practice yoga in the hope of realizing our deep desire for fulfilment. It is a science, or rather an art, that helps us to free ourselves from what we mistakenly believe ourselves to be. The basis of all yoga is attention, listening, silent observation, seeing and hearing without being lost in what is seen, what is heard. In the mirror of your mind things appear and disappear. Be alert, see this without becoming implicated, then you will discover yourself in this permanent observation and you will find peace and security.

The ultimate end—if there is one—is to free yourself from this identification with the person. Hitherto you have always surrounded yourself with imagined limitations, you have imposed images on yourself. This conditioning is the root of all mistakes and brings suffering to you and to others. Sooner or later, your physical and psychological resources will be exhausted. Reduced to despair, the question "Who am I" will arise within you, and you will at long last find the answer. A living answer.

I yearn for a life free from upheaval, to be free of this constant swinging back and forth between pleasure and suffering. Is there a state of permanent plenitude free from all strife?

You are what is permanent, you cannot leave it, even for a minute. You can find yourself free from thought but you can never cease being what you are fundamentally. Things that incessantly change can never lead you towards what you are essentially: unchangeable and encompassing all change. Changes only belong to the mind. What do you expect to achieve through them? No effort can lead you to this ultimate harmony, every attempt leads you further away. Only discernment gives rise to the awakening of this understanding.

How can I convince myself of the uselessnes of all effort?

As long as you think you can achieve freedom by thinking, all your acts will be motivated by fear, anxiety or desire. There is no end to things, your problems and suffering will continue to accumulate. In the thought-action process, acts motivated by fear will only bring you back to your starting point, thus enclosing you within a vicious circle. See the futility of wanting to modify, to change or "get out of it." Seeing, no longer influenced by the past or the projected future, is global vision.

You must leave behind you the idea of improving. There is nothing to be found, nothing to achieve. Searching and wanting to achieve something are the fuel for the entity you believe yourself to be. Don't project an idea of reality, of freedom. Be simply aware of the facts of your existence without wanting change. Seeing things in this way will bring you a state of deep relaxation both physical and psychological. Even this state becomes an object of perception and dissolves in your observation where there is no longer observer or state observed.

Are you conscious during the deep sleep state?

The question shows a fundamental misunderstanding. Consciousness is not found in any state. Deep sleep is found in consciousness. Deep sleep is closer to your natural non-state than the waking or dreaming states because it is without ego, not in the subject/object relation. The experience of deep sleep is a profound reminder of our being. This reminder is still an organic memory because all our physical structure is struck by the peace of living in non-volition. This reminder of presence invites us to inquire, to meditate.

So the invitation from the deep sleep state leaves us longing for non-dual living in all the states?

Yes. It is only in the waking state that we can face our dual existence but we can also come to the insight of non-duality during the dreaming state.

But does this insight last?

We can be deeply struck so that it leaves its effect in us, but the strongest insights come in the states before waking or in the waking state.

But what is this insight you are talking about?

It is an instantaneous apperception that your total being is always present, always in the "now." As our psychosomatic structure is affected by the insight we qualify it as peace, joy, plenitude, but these are symbols, pointers to describe an experience which is lived beyond description. An "apple" is not an apple!

How can I master my imagination? In other words how can I govern my mind?

This mind is an extension of our being, therefore it can only function harmoniously when illuminated by it. All forms of control submit us to memory. A controlled mind can never act freely, nor spontaneously. Of course we can say that memory, experience, is the best of all tools in the relative world, but it is insufficient for knowing what is beyond it, for it functions within the framework of the already known. The unknown is the closest to us, too near to be perceived. It is closer than picking a flower as the Upanishads say.

By clear-sighted awareness of cause and effect, another view of things, a new dimension of life, will be opened to you.

*How can I come to a deeper quest so that I can convince myself that
"I Am"?*

The conviction comes from the "I am." There is an original
desire in you to be yourself knowingly. This desire is fed all
your life by deep sleep and moments of utter tranquility. The
desire to be never leaves you, so welcome it and follow it as
you would follow a mountain stream to its source. You would
never try to change the course of the stream or in any way
interfere with it. You remain only its companion. So be the
close companion of your deepest longing. It will inevitably
bring you to your heart's desire.

Ultimate desire is living without desire, where there is
no longer any room for the idea of being somebody. Let this
become clear within you. Be completely earnest. Live it with
all your heart. Be intimately familiar with the certainty that
absolutely nothing perceived can possibly guarantee bliss.

*How can we destroy this illusion that makes us believe we are the
person?*

You will recognize this illusion through investigation.
Everything you take to be personal, everything the I creates
or repeats, is false. Liberation consists in being free from
the me. Understanding this is instantaneous, total, without
return. It is a sudden opening to a new dimension which
leaves us in silent plenitude where there is no one who claims
and no one who suffers.

*When I find myself before you, I am in a state of wonder. I can no
longer feel or formulate all the questions that seemed vital to me a
moment ago.*

When one is struck by wonder or astonishment there is perfect nonduality between the knower and the thing known. It is living reality. Let yourself be totally absorbed by it, then thought and action will derive directly from this wonderment which is the background, your natural state.

I feel hemmed in by mediocrity; life seems very dreary to me.

Something that is happening at the present moment, or something you remember, both appear within awareness. When you think of the present moment it is already part of the past. So all your qualifications and feelings about life are already past. Problems, weariness, boredom, depression stem only from the mistaken notion of taking ourselves for a certain person with certain ideas, a particular background, etc. Our difficulties come when our projections into the future in the hope of attaining some result are thwarted. We choose the results and goals we think best but it is a choice entirely dependent on our likes and dislikes, our personal conditioning, our attitudes. Thus, no matter how many objects we collect, how much accumulated learning or experience, we are inevitably locked into the round of pleasure and suffering. Only when we live in our wholeness, free from the person, free from all goals, preference and choice, can there be a full expression of life. When we live without qualifying we live in the moment, the eternal present "now." Here, in the absence of thoughts of the past and longings for the future, we are in our fullness. From fullness flows love and all actions come out of love.

Unthinkable Presence is your real nature in which all appears. Because you identify with your thoughts instead of presence, you feel limited, restricted. In freeing yourself from this restriction you come to live your limitlessness. Then everything that happens in your life will have new meaning.

*I*n his life a man can ask himself many questions but they all revolve around one question: "Who am I?" All questions stem from this one. So that the answer to "Who am I?" is the answer to all questions, the ultimate answer. But we must be quite clear about certain things, so that we don't appropriate this question as just another idea among many.

A man always speaks of himself as an I and gives this I many roles: I run, I eat, I'm hungry, I'm sitting, sleeping. All these activities refer to the body he firmly believes himself to be. He also says: I remember, I think, I'm surprised, worried, etc., etc. Thus he also takes himself to be his thoughts. Here the I-image identifies with the body and the mind. But if we observe things more closely, we soon come to realize that it is the body that is doing the acting and the mind the thinking. These are the tools of consciousness which function without an I-image.

Our mental and physical activities constantly change throughout the four stages of life. These experiences prove that there is an experiencer who recalls the experiences when stimulated. But what must be clearly seen is that the recalling, like the event itself, is a present happening. The thought of a past is a present thought. This continual presentness is what we mean by saying consciousness is one with its object. Memory and change are thus fundamentally illusions which dissolve in presence. All recalling takes place in this timeless,

145

unchanging background. The experiencer is one with this background.

We can only know and remember what we have already experienced, something that happened to us, a thought we had, or something we did. When actually thinking or doing, there is only thinking or doing, nothing else. In the moment of doing something there is no doer. The mind and the object of its perception are not two. The world and the mind are not different. They are discontinuous but appear in the present continuum which is silent awareness, so that in the end we could say that everything is awareness.

In the state of deep sleep, the ego is not involved and the body and brain continue to function. There is only the pure awareness that is present when the I-image is absent, when we are free from all thought constructs.

It is from this awareness that statements arise such as "I slept well." Consciousness is its own light, it does not need a vehicle. Objects, on the contrary, depend entirely on consciousness. They could not otherwise be perceived. Consciousness knows itself by itself. Once we clearly recognize this truth we are freed from our mental framework and the true I knowingly reveals itself.

The question "Who am I?" springs from the "I am." The reply is already present before we even ask the question, the question in fact originates in the answer.

The question itself, on the level on which it is asked, the level of conflict, cannot give rise to a reply, for when we look at it more closely, we cannot possibly put the answer into words, even less think of it. However, the driving force pushing us on to find an answer by means of thought finally dies away, and is reabsorbed into the eternal, all-answering presence, I am.

But when wake up and say "I have slept well" am I not only refer-ring to a feeling of relaxation?

That is true but there is something more in saying this than just feeling the body is relaxed. There is a delicious sensation of wellbeing that comes from being bathed in sweetness itself.

Look, when someone asks you, "Are you alive? Are you conscious?" you immediately say "Yes" without having to think. You don't refer to any feeling or representation first. This spontaneous "Yes" comes from the deep conviction that you are consciousness.

If we cannot proceed towards understanding, how does it just happen?

Any form of exercise is bound to a goal, to a result. But this is an obstacle when there is no goal to be reached since what you are looking for is here now and always has been. When the mind is free from all desire to become, it is at peace and attention spontaneously shifts from the object to the ultimate "subject," a foretaste of your real Self. Be vigilant, clear-sighted, aware of your constant desire to be this or that and don't make any effort. What you are is without direction so all direction takes you away from knowingly being what you are. In this letting go of all trying, time no longer exists, there is no more expectation. In the absence of name and form what room is there for fear and insecurity? When there is no projection there is the forefeeling of wholeness.

Does maturity come from inquiry or does inquiry come out of maturity?

Maturity comes out of inquiring. Inquiring is natural to us, look at babies and young children. Unfortunately society and the educational system do not foster this inherent exploration and the child often becomes bored. We are taught to superimpose the past on the present and future and so we lose the excitement, the newness of the moment. It takes alertness to see this mechanical functioning.

You may have a glimpse that every moment is unique and you will spontaneously be brought back to the background of real inquiry: attention, openness. This inquiry is not localized as a concept or a percept. It is free from anticipation, expectation and becoming. When you clearly see things around you as they are in relation with the whole of your being, there is ripening. You see the false as simply false without wasting time and energy analyzing why it is false, defending or explaining it. It just no longer belongs to you. You are out of it. You feel yourself in an atmosphere of clarity. Here, the inquiry of the truth-seeker transcends that of the child. While the child still focuses on the object of inquiry, the mature seeker focuses on the inquiring itself, and one day discovers himself *to be* the inquiring.

Even if one becomes independent from one's social conditioning— family, education, etc.—is there not a fundamental "condition" that belongs to being human, that has to do with biological survival through the ages?

I agree there is always a certain amount of cultural and biological conditioning. This belongs to our existence. Being free does not mean you negate, eliminate by will or refuse this conditioning. It means you are not identified with it, stuck in it. You don't try to free yourself because you know yourself to be free. So there is no reaction against the past, against the society. To a certain extent your functions are within the conditioning. You don't spend energy trying to accept it because it doesn't concern your real self. To know that you are not you know what you are not. So you know your mechanism, you are familiar with your conditioning, but because you are not bound to it it presents no restriction.

Humanity has inhabited the globe for millions of years but freedom and love have never changed nor been conditioned. Freedom and love are beyond thinking and representation, time and space.

When we live in waiting, in openness, what is the stimulation for action to occur? How could any action at all come about? In other words how can the arrow shoot itself and find its target without a shooter?

First we must see that we cannot will ourselves to be open because openness is our very nature. Any tiny residue of willing, of wanting to be open takes us away from what we are. Willing never goes beyond willing. So the only way to be free from this circle is to glimpse the truth that openness is the egoless state, that it is here and now.

This openness is free from all center and periphery; it is without a controller, an observer, one who chooses or decides. All functioning takes place spontaneously. In observation free from an observer, the observed appears and disappears without memory interfering. To take your example of archery, this means that the target and the position and state of the body and arrow are all witnessed without goal or intention. At a certain moment the right elements come together and the arrow is spontaneously released, but there is no one who lets it go. When there is no shooter it is the non-state of the man of Tao whose perfect relaxation in the midst of action lets in the flow of Tao.

Does this mean that unless we have experienced our openness we cannot act correctly?

Yes, because until then only the mind acts. We cannot act rightly or accurately from memory because no situation ever repeats. Every shooting, every meeting is new. Right acting comes out of the moment itself.

What about codes of behavior, legal, social and moral or religious which teach us a way to behave and say we can learn how to apply this behavior appropriately in all situations?

Codified action is never moral.

But our society is not ready for spontaneous living...

It is true. For the moment we need crutches but one day we will be free from crutches. Right social behavior calls for sensitivity but when there is no sensitivity we need rules, but what you use as a crutch must become obvious to you.

You mean we must know our crutches?

Exactly. Don't lose yourself in them, in patterns. Inquiry will bring you to know what is a crutch, what is memory and what belongs to the creative moment.

Doesn't codified behavior often appear as good and wise as spontaneous right acting?

Maybe. But when you see learned action there are moments of wrong emphasis which do not come from the flow of spontaneity. Only someone in the light can see this clearly.

You have said that we must transpose our understanding into daily life. What is the difference between doing this and practicing a learned social behavior?

First we have to see that in daily life we don't act according to our understanding. When you see the false as false, what remains is truth.

I need to be clearer about this. Once there is a glimpse of truth, once the principle has been seen: that we are not what we think and what we are appears in clarity, then certain elements of our life shift spontaneously, rearrange, drop away, what you call a reorchestration of our energies, is this so?

Yes.

But still are there not other areas, more dense and complicated, that need more time to become integrated? Don't we need some effort here in transposing understanding into life?

It is not effort, it is intelligence which functions. This intelligence belongs to your effortless openness. A single glimpse of truth can stimulate this intelligence. Transposition occurs through analogy, transposing understanding on one plane to another plane. What the archer learns in his art can be transposed to all areas of his life. The art of archery is only a tool for analogy.

A key to the art of living?

Yes. The way we do body-work is also a key. The approach to your body on the physical plane, being completely open to the perception, must be transposed to all areas of life.

Taoism seems to be going with the flow of life, Yoga seems to master the flow of life. Perhaps they are ultimately not different but as far as the traditions go, what would you say are the differences? Can the way of mastery, the way of power, ever bring one to freedom? It seems that our present society is founded on this belief, that control can bring harmony.

Let us first make clear what is meant by "going with the flow of life." When you are identified with a person, an idea, a body which you believe you are, then there is object/object relation. In this relation you can never see how the ocean of life solicits you. You cannot be adequate to the coming and going of the waves. Your action and non-action is inevitable reaction because you live in images, in the mind. You act or don't act according to certain motives, certain morality, certain ideologies or spiritual ideas. You don't really accept life, but rather submit to it. Then there is fatalism. Fatalism only exists on the level of living as an individual, a personal entity.

Really going with the flow of life is "passive-active," passive in that the ego, the personality is completely absent, there is no intention, will, goal or motive. But active in that in the absence of the ego you live in your presence, your awareness and all your energies and talents are liberated. You are alert, adequate to every situation, always vigilant, ready for anything. It is a state without choice, where action appears out of the situation and non-action also appears as action. In awareness there is no thought of action or not, you simply function in the moment itself.

Regarding Yoga, Yoga is an Indian system, a discipline completely founded on duality. This dual system can never bring you to the non-dual non-state. It can, however, bring you to see that you are in a dual system and in seeing it you are out of it. But I was introduced to another, unorthodox, way of seeing yoga when I met a swami in India in the 1950's and asked him what he understood by "yoga." He gave an answer that astonished me; he said, "It means sitting right." Then he added "walking right and right doing." For him, yoga was not about asanas and kundalini, it meant sitting according to the chair and acting according to the situation! So we can say that from the ultimate point of view, letting life flow in your alertness and being adequate in all circumstances are exactly the same.

Our society today emphasizes the fractional personality which is the origin of competition, achieving, aggression, war. We are encouraged to be more and more specialized. It takes us away from our real global nature. But domination, assertion and manipulation can never bring wisdom and a healthy society. On the contrary, the light of wisdom, love and harmony is concealed by the personality and its qualifications. Our society is living in the dark. But love and wisdom are infinitely patient, unchanged, ever there since before time.

Is there any difference between the mystical state of unity in which subject and object dissolve, and the non-state in which subject and object dissolve?

In the mystical approach the devotee receives from God the movement towards God. In the direct approach the inquiry into what we are not comes from what we are. In both there is a coming back to where we originally belong. In both, on the phenomenal plane, there is gratitude and thanking.

But for the mystic isn't there always a feeling of gratitude to God?

In this case the mystic has remained in relation, adorer to adored. In a certain way there is still somebody. In the highest unity this adorer, this somebody, is no longer present. There is only God. As Meister Eckhart said, "God is when you are not."

The inquirer lives in the openness of the inquiring that comes from the answer itself. This openness can never be an object, a perception, a state. It is free from all assertion.

What is the last object to dissolve?

The last and the first is the idea of being somebody. The blank state and all subtle states stem from this idea.

What do you mean by "blank state"?

In the blank state the object has dissolved but the subject/ object relation remains, so the object is potentially still there. In other words the absence of the object is still an object. This is the inevitable result of progressive elimination by will.

You have said that the real meeting is after the meeting, but cannot there be a timeless non-state in the meeting between two lovers for example?

The content of the meeting on the phenomenal plane comes to its integration when there is no me and therefore no other. There may be rare occasions when this integration occurs during the meeting but since events on the physical plane occur in succession and are bound to time and space, the totality of the meeting appears only in the absence of these restrictions. It lives in its fullness in your timeless awareness.

How do you distinguish between pure perception and direct perception?

In a direct perception you are one with the seen. In a pure perception, the perception empties itself in the homeground, seeing, so you are one with the seeing.

When the disciple becomes autonomous what is his relation with his guru? Does he always feel gratitude? What state is the disciple in when he feels independent but no real gratitude?

In the practical (as opposed to the theoretical) approach, there is no disciple and no teacher. If there were there could be no transmission of being, of oneness. There would only be teaching on the mental level.

The disciple hears from his guru that he is not the body, senses and mind so he temporarily stops emphasizing these and focuses on what he is. After he is established in his real nature, body, senses and mind are integrated in the completeness of being and they carry with them the "stamp" of the guru. There remains a current of love and friendship and gratitude for the transmission of the flame, the primordial gift.

Someone who feels independent *from* anything lives in reaction. At this moment he is not a disciple. To forget the guru is to forget himself.

Who is the knower of my true nature?

Your real nature is knowing. It cannot be known. All that the mind can know is not you. Your "I" becomes a living reality once the idea that society has given you of being a separate entity has entirely left you—together with its desires, fears and imagination, its belief that it is this or that. One reminder, one foretaste of your unrestricted being will immediately make it clear that these are not reality but its expressions. You will be instantaneously convinced of what you are. The truth of the nature of existence will be spontaneously revealed to you: that *you* give birth to all that exists. Without awareness nothing would be. What is experienced on a phenomenal plane is not you but an extension of you. Experience is in you but you are not experience.

In living freedom you are free from choice, free from striving, free from the need to define or qualify yourself in any way. Everything that exists appears in consciousness, but consciousness is not lost in existence. I cannot prove this to you in words nor can any second-hand information convince you. Make this a living proof and you will find your still home-ground. Then there is only thankfulness where no one thanks.

You are neither this nor that. You are the knower of all, primal perception, original limitless being.

Printed in the United States
113126LV00002B/111/A

9 780955 176272